REVD JOHN WYNDHAM

THE CROSS AND THE RAILWAY

ANGLICAN MINISTRY
ALONG THE TRANS
AUSTRALIA RAILWAY

Ark House Press
arkhousepress.com

© 2023 Revd John Wyndham

All rights reserved. Apart from any fair dealing for the purpose of study, research, criticism, or review, as permitted under the Copyright Act, no part may be reproduced by any process without written permission.

Unless otherwise stated, all Scriptures are taken from the New International Translation (Holy Bible. Copyright© 1996, 2004, 2007, 2013 by Tyndale House Foundation. Used by permission of Tyndale House Publishers Inc., Carol Stream, Illinois 60188. All rights reserved.)

Some names and identifying details have been changed to protect the privacy of individuals.

Cataloguing in Publication Data:
Title: The Cross and the Railway
ISBN: 9780645880939 (pbk)
Subjects: REL108020 [RELIGION / Christian Church / History]; REL012170 [RELIGION / Christian Living / Personal Memoirs]; REL012140 [RELIGION / Christian Living / Calling & Vocation];
Other Authors/Contributors: Wyndham, Revd John;

Design by initiateagency.com

for

Jan who shared the adventure with me;

the women and men – nurses, doctors, pilots and others - who served with the Church of England Flying Medical Service;

the railway workers and station owners who welcomed me and responded the ministry.

PREFACE

The completion of the manuscript for this book coincides with the 60th anniversary of my becoming a member of the Bush Church Aid Society field staff in outback South Australia.

I have drawn the material from a variety of sources, some of which have been acknowledged in the endnotes. Much of it comes from my memory or from prayer letters that we sent. Some of it has come from articles I have read on the Internet.

If you wonder about the details of the times when trains arrived and departed, apart from those at Tarcoola which governed our daily life, I have drawn that from a copy of the Commonwealth Railways working timetable which I still have. I have put the distances in miles because that is what they were at the time. However, in most instances I have put the metric equivalent in brackets. All the photographs except the cover are mine.

It was an amazing walk with God over 4½ years at Ceduna, Minnipa and Tarcoola in South Australia; at Norseman in Western Australia.

It involved ministry in the towns, to farming communities, to grazing properties along the Eyre Highway from Kyancutta SA to Norseman WA, along the entire length of the Trans Australia Railway, to sheep/cattle stations north and south of the railway together with a chaplaincy at the Atomic Weapons Research Establishment, Maralinga.

It was ministry to "all sorts and conditions of men [women and children]" as the 1662 Book of Common Prayer puts it.

It follows the deeds of pioneers beginning with those who built the railway together with Methodist lay pastor Mr Caust and his successors. That pioneer spirit continued with the early clergy of the Bush Church Aid Society, the nurses who staffed the hospitals, the development of regular ministry along the Trans Australia Railway and the establishment of the Tarcoola Mission District which fulfilled a dream BCA founder S.J Kirkby had in 1921.

It was lonely at times but rewarding as God moved in the hearts of people and changed lives.

To Him be the glory!

John Wyndham
February 2023

FOREWORD

"The Cross and the Railway" is a very worthwhile read. It is an illuminating and engrossing story for anyone with even the mildest interest in the work of God in the more remote parts of Australia. John Wyndham has created an account in which the reader will sense something of the challenges and joys of a very particular ministry.

The Bush Church Aid Society, and people like John, have played, and are playing, a unique role in the continuing mission of the Lord Jesus Christ to 'outback' Australia

John has created an account of Christian ministry along the great and famous East-West Railway Line, and the territory surrounding it, that allows the reader to share something of the adventure, exhilaration, disappointments and rewards of that work. Having had, for a time, a very small part in that work, as well as a ministry connection with John, I can personally commend his account to any reader.

Read "The Cross and the Railway" to expand your knowledge of what God has done "along the Line" and let it prompt your prayers and support of those who continue God's mission on this great continent.

Thank you John for opening up this mission field for your readers.

The Rt Revd. Harry Goodhew
Former Archbishop of Sydney

1.

THE TRANS AUSTRALIA RAILWAY[1]

The Trans Australia Railway connected the eastern states with Western Australia. It was one of the first major infrastructure projects following Federation in 1901, With a survey completed in 1909, the Commonwealth Government authorised the construction of the railway in December 1911. The cost was estimated at £4,045,000 [$8,090.000]. The railway line was built to the standard gauge of 4ft 8½ in [1,435 mm], even though the state railway systems at both ends were the narrow gauge of 3ft 6in [1066.8mm].

The route went north from Port Augusta to Pimba and then west to what became known as Tarcoola Siding, south of the now abandoned Tarcoola gold mining town. Continuing west it passed through the mallee covered sandhills of the southern bulge of the Great Victoria Desert to Ooldea at the eastern end of the Nullarbor Plain which it crossed on the way to Kalgoorlie. The total length of the railway was 1036½ miles [1658.4 km]. The Nullarbor stretch included 298¾ miles [478 km] of dead-straight track from west of Ooldea to Nurina in WA - the world's longest stretch of railway without a bend.

During construction, reservoirs for water were built ranging in size from 3 to 8 million gallons [13.5 to 36 million litres]. Food supplies for the navvies were also provided. These supplies were transported by a weekly Slow Mixed Goods train called the "Bread and Butter" [later known as "*Tea & Sugar*"].

The governments of South Australia and Western Australia each ceded one eighth of a mile [203 metres] of land on either side of the route to the Federal government. Work commenced from Port Augusta in September 1912 and from Kalgoorlie in February 2013. Construction materials were delivered daily, initially by camel and then by rail as the line progressed. The two parts of the railway met on 17 October 1917.

Commonwealth Railways was established by an Act of Parliament to operate the railway and the first train departed Port Augusta on 22 October 1917. The time for the journey from Port Augusta to Kalgoorlie was set at 37 hours 20 minutes inclusive of stops; the reverse journey was ten minutes longer. The average speed was 30mph [approx.49kph][2].

Towns of 20-30 houses and other buildings were established at Kingoonya, Tarcoola, Cook and Rawlinna (WA). They also had post offices. The four towns had railway stations without platforms and passengers descended from carriages by steps[3]. Settlements for permanent way workers and their families, commonly known as fettler camps, were built approximately 50 miles [80km] apart, each comprising six or twelve 3-bedroom houses.

Each gang of fettlers was responsible for the track 25 miles on either side of their settlement. The settlements were named after Australian prime ministers, governors-general and other notable people or had aboriginal names. There were also some single men's camps each comprising three huts with two bedrooms and a common kitchen/dining/lounge area[4].

A telephone line connecting all railway towns and camps to Port Augusta was erected beside the railway. This allowed control of operations along the single track, rather like the staff systems employed in more populated areas. There will more about this in the next chapter.

State government primary schools were built outside the railway reserves at Kingoonya, Tarcoola and Cook in South Australia as well as at Rawlinna in WA. Tarcoola, officially known as Tarcoola South because of the gold mining township, had a police station with cells, a hotel, a community hall and a church building on state land. Cook had two lock-ups – 8 feet square galvanised iron huts[5]. Kingoonya also had a hotel. Eventually, permanent hospitals were erected at Cook and Tarcoola with a medical clinic/hostel at Rawlinna. These medical facilities were staffed by nursing sisters of the Bush Church Aid Society and were part of what became the network of the Church of England Flying Medical Service.

Coal dumps were established approximately 100 miles [160km] apart at Pimba, Kingoonya [initially], Tarcoola, Barton (in the sand hills) Cook, Reid, Rawlinna and Zanthus. Water reservoirs for the trains were also built at these locations. Supplies of coal and water were brought by special trains. These towns/settlements each had large crew rest houses built of stone for drivers, firemen and guards to stay in at the end of their shifts. Tarcoola, Cook and Rawlinna had engine sheds and other work sheds as well as rail triangles in place of turntables to enable locomotives to be turned around[6].

Freight yards were built at Port Augusta and Parkeston east of Kalgoorlie. The line was later extended south from Port Augusta to Port Pirie where a large freight terminal was established.

The initial passenger rolling stock was 65 feet [19.91 metres] long carriages with sleeping accommodation. There were also dining cars and a lounge car for first-class passengers. The passenger locomotives chosen were of a similar type to the New South Wales Government Railways C32

Class and known as Commonwealth Railways "G" Class. The goods or freight locomotives were basically those of the NSW Railways D50 Class and were classified as Commonwealth Railways "K" Class[7].

Replacement of steam locomotives by diesel electric locomotives began in September 1951. Constructed by Clyde Engineering in NSW these locos were known as GM Class and 47 were built.

The GMs only needed to be refueled at Cook which cut down on the time for both passenger and freight operations. There was no air conditioning on passenger trains until the GMs along with sealed steel carriages were introduced[8].

Fast Goods trains, certainly after World War II, carried large lorries or semi-trailers on flat top wagons which enabled them to avoid wear and tear on the narrow, unsealed Eyre Highway. For much of its length, the highway was only a dirt track along which there was no reliable water supply for 770 miles [1232 km] between Ceduna SA and Norseman WA, There were few repair facilities and very expensive fuel – more than double the price in Adelaide[9].

2.
COMMUNICATIONS ALONG THE LINE

There were two methods of communication for rail workers along the Trans Australia Railway. One was the weekly Slow Mixed Goods train nicknamed the *Tea and Sugar*. The other was the dedicated telephone line mentioned in the previous chapter.

The *Tea and Sugar* was the "life line" of the Railway. It was the sole source of provisions for the isolated settlements. There were two trains; the forward journey of one began before the other returned to Port Augusta.

Train #527, with a maximum speed of 40mph [64kph], the *Tea and Sugar* departed Port Augusta on Thursday mornings and stabled overnight at Pimba, Barton, Cook, Loongana, Rawlinna and Zanthus before arriving at Parkeston, the goods yard three miles east of Kalgoorlie, on the following Wednesday morning at 11:30 [if it was not delayed]. On the return journey, as Train #514, known as the *Bomber*, it departed Parkeston the next day at 4:05am. It only had three scheduled stops, Rawlinna, Cook and Tarcoola but stopped at other settlements as required. It crossed the other westbound *Tea and Sugar* at Cook on Saturday arriving back at Port Augusta on Monday evening.

The *Tea and Sugar* was brought into existence in 1915 as a provisions train for workers constructing the railway. They and their families depended on the train for every necessity since the rail link was the only form of transport into the region. By the time the railway was completed in 1917, as we have seen, settlements had been established along the route at which many railway operations, locomotive maintenance and track repair employees lived with their families who needed food, water and other goods transported to them.

On each journey, the *Tea and Sugar* comprised carriages/wagons to suit the different needs of residents. There was the Butcher's Van, a pay/bank van and a post office van. Before refrigerated vans were introduced, live sheep were carried on the train and the butcher slaughtered them on the overnight stops which meant that people were able to buy fresh meat.

While Tarcoola, Cook and Rawlinna had general stores, folk at the other settlements used to fill out an order form for groceries, fruit and vegetables. The orders were made up in Port Augusta and boxed with the name of the settlement and the name of the employee. Payment was deducted from wages. The boxes were delivered weekly. Perishables such as butter were stored in a chillroom and added to the order on site. Clothes could be ordered and there were also homemade baby clothes for sale. In December there was a Christmas car with a much-anticipated Santa who brought presents for the children.

The Welfare Car, an old carriage painted white, was attached as necessary. It was used by Child Welfare nursing sisters who made quarterly visits to check on the health of children along the Line. As well, a dentist made half yearly visits and clergy used it. The Welfare Car was divided into two sections. The front half was a waiting room/meeting room. A corridor ran along the left-hand side of the of the other half of the carriage off which there were two sleeping cabins, a shower, a toilet, a kitchenette and a room for consultations. Those using the Welfare Car were given complimentary first-class passes.

Former Commissioner of South Australian Railways, Dr Ron Fitch who was the chief engineer for the Trans Australia Railway early in his career, once commented that the *Tea and Sugar* was the "*most over-glamorised train in Australia ... whose real claim to fame was that its start-to-stop average speed must have made it the slowest train in the world*"[10].

The dedicated telephone line was one of several strung on poles beside the railway. It connected the traffic controllers at Port Augusta with Kalgoorlie and the various settlements. There were phone boxes at each end of the crossing loops so that both driver and guard could speak with Port Augusta and receive orders to proceed on the single track. Other communication lines included the PMG[11] phone lines between Adelaide and Perth and the ABC[12] landline. There were electro-magnetic repeaters at Tarcoola, Cook and Rawlinna with technicians at Tarcoola.

At the commencement of journeys from Port Augusta and Kalgoorlie/Parkeston, the crew would be given an initial train order [instructions] authorising them to proceed along a section of about 100 miles [160 km] with a proviso to report at an intervening siding. This meant that if they were running late, they would wait for a train coming the other way. Each train order had to be written in a book of duplicate forms. The forms had space for the train number, the locomotive number(s) and the destination as well as the names of the driver and guard. The crews kept the originals

There were phones in each ganger's house[13] and the gangs had portable phones which could be connected to the line at the location where they were working. This was a security measure which enabled the gangs to know if a train was running ahead of time, or if there was an emergency. These portable phones were connected by a long wooden pole with brass arms at one end which were fitted over the two wires.

Initially, the PMG lines supplemented the East-West Telegraph Line which opened in 1877. That telegraph line made communication between Adelaide and Perth possible with use of Morse Code signals which had to be transcribed at each station before being retransmitted. These stations were at Port Augusta, Port Lincoln, Fowlers Bay, Eucla and Albany. The telegraph line was finally closed in 1927 when additional telephone lines were added beside the railway line.

3.
EARLY CHRISTIAN MINISTRY

While information about early ministry along the Trans Australia Railway is sparse, there are some snippets available from which conclusions can be drawn.

Gold was discovered on Wilgena sheep station in 1893 by a shearing shed hand named Nichols. There was little development before 1900. A post office opened on 18 August 1900 and a town was proclaimed on 21 February 1901. It was named after *Tarcoola*, the winner of the 1893 Melbourne Cup horse race. The horse had been bred at Tarcoola sheep station on the Darling River in New South Wales. Tarcoola is an aboriginal word meaning *bend in the river*.

By mid-1901 there were at least 300-400 men at Tarcoola and from the following newspaper report, the Methodist Church of South Australia decided to provide ministry.

> "*The first United Methodist Conference in South Australia appointed Mr. Caust to the Kapunda circuit, where he was well received and very useful. Some 300 to 400 men had gone to Tarcoola, and as no other provision was made to meet their*

spiritual needs, the president, the Rev. Dr. Burgess, sent him to the field"[14].

His journey to Tarcoola was adventurous, to say the least –

"Mr. Caust went by train to Port Augusta, where the leading residents, including the Church of England minister, evinced deep interest in his mission. He rode his bicycle the 300 miles to Tarcoola. On the way he held services at various {sheep} stations, bush pubs and a copper mine. Something more than the novelty of the thing led all those in reach to attend. In one case there were three commercial travellers, two Afghans, two publicans, a brewer and several blacks present, and one of the publicans made the collection. After many romantic incidents, in one instance going 30 miles out of his way, Mr. Caust reached Tarcoola"[15].

On arrival in Tarcoola, Mr Caust seems to have set about his task with enthusiasm, getting to know people socially, preaching the Gospel, ministering to those in need and taking funerals.

"Believing in being all things to all men, that by all means, he might have some, he joined in cricket, at which he is an expert, and other innocent games, and thus won the sympathy of the men. For the most part the services were held in bush tents, and were occasionally interrupted by the interjections of strange men, who were answered in such a manner that they did not repeat the action. Sometimes the cooks brought their potatoes to the place, sat behind the preacher and peeled them during the sermon. Two sermons were preached on 'The Camel', rather an unpromising subject, as it had but one

> *head, though possessing many points, especially when in poor condition. The frequent kneeling of the camel, its patience in bearing burdens, its great services to man, etc., were all aptly used to teach spiritual lessons which awakened deep interest. The sick were visited, and the dying pointed to the living Christ. The funerals, with two camels followed by rough men walking two and two, were deeply solemn, and strong men wept as the impressive burial service was read. At length Mr. Caust was stricken with fever, and at one time appeared in dangerous condition*"[16].

From the same newspaper report, the Church of England provided a visiting ministry from the parish of Port Augusta which also included care of Mr Caust during his illness.

> *"Fortunately the Rev. Mr. Dowdney, M.A. Church of England minister of Port Augusta, was on a visit to the field at the time. He nursed Mr. Caust through the worst part of his illness, and his fraternal support was greatly appreciated"*[17].

By August 1902, the Methodist ministry was obviously firmly established. Adelaide newspaper *The Advertiser* had two items that month:

> *"TARCOOLA.*
>
> *August 4.-To-day an iron store, bought by the Methodists for use as a church, was removed to a central position in the town. The Rev. George Johnstone is the clergyman in charge, and he has announced that the building will be formally opened on Sunday"*[18].

> "TARCOOLA.
>
> August 14 - The opening of the new Methodist Church was celebrated by a concert and coffee social. Songs, duets, and recitations were contributed by lady and gentlemen amateurs. There was a large attendance"[19].

A further newspaper report in the following month implies that Church of England ministry had become more permanent when the Bishop of Adelaide, The Right Revd John Harmer, appointed lay readers.

> "An organ is to be obtained for the Church of England, as regular services are now being held at the Government battery. They are conducted by lay readers, appointed by the bishop."[20]

As the railway line was built and finally operational it would be feasible to believe that the ministry extended to those working on the project. The Methodist Church eventually established a Tarcoola Circuit which certainly existed until 1928 when the second of two memorial plaques in the Tarcoola church building was erected. It seems that one or both men died while serving the community. It also seems that the church building was moved from the gold town to near the railway line when, or before, mining ceased around 1918. The galvanised iron church eventually had fibro lining. The "manse" was a two-room annex[21].

I do not know how far along the Line the Methodist clergy ministered between 1917 and 1928 when the last pastor died in office. However, it is probable that they went east as far as Pimba and west to at least Cook as the Commonwealth Railways Act. allowed ministers of religion to travel at 25% of the first-class fare and their equipment at 25% of the freight rates[22].

There is little record of what ministry took place along the Line over the next ten years, but given the generous fare for clergy, there would have been some. Church of England clergy from Port Augusta occasionally visited Tarcoola and the surrounding sheep stations but probably did not go much further afield. Roman Catholic priests visited Tarcoola at least once a year.

Heine Noack was a Lutheran pastor in the Riverlands district who had a burden for the lost. For about twenty years from the mid-1950s, he made two ministry trips a year along the Trans Australia Railway and the Central Australia Railway [the original "*Ghan*"]. He travelled in the Welfare Car attached to the *Tea and Sugar* which meant that he only had limited time in each fettler camp. During those visits he distributed evangelistic tracts he had written[23].

4.
BCA GETS INVOLVED

The Bush Church Aid Society was founded in 1919 as a Church of England (now the Anglican Church of Australia) missionary society to provide ministry in outback Australia. It succeeded the work of the English Colonial and Continental Church Society which had provided ministry in Perth from the 1830s.

BCA was the vision of The Revd Stanley James Kirkby, then rector of St Anne's Ryde (Sydney), and later second Co-adjutor Bishop of Sydney. S.J. Kirkby became the first Organising Missioner.

BCA's motto, "*Australia for Christ.*" defined its aim –

> "*to go out and serve the people of Australia in places where they are not able in the ordinary way, to provide a ministry for their spiritual welfare, …*"[24].

Initially, BCA provided only parish clergy but the ministry expanded to include school children's hostels together with medical work at Cann River in Victoria and Ceduna. Eventually, after the Church of England Flying Medical Service was established, cottage hospitals were built at

BCA GETS INVOLVED

Tarcoola and Cook together with the medical hostel at Rawlinna on the Trans Australia Railway.

Several books have been written detailing the history of the Bush Church Aid Society[25] and I do not intend to duplicate their text except where necessary. This to be mainly a reflection on pastoral ministry along the Trans Line.

In 1920, the Bishop of Willochra, the Rt Revd Gilbert White, asked the new Bush Church Aid Society to provide a clergyman to serve a mission district based at Ceduna. To be known as the Far West Coast Mission District, it was detached from the parish of Streaky Bay. The Revd Neville Haviland answered the call and was appointed Priest in Charge of Ceduna in 1921.

The new mission district extended west to Eucla, 300 miles away just over the border with Western Australia. During his six years of ministry, Neville probably regularly visited Fowlers Bay which, as previously mentioned, had a telegraph station and was the port for farms and isolated sheep stations west of Ceduna. He may also have visited the telegraph station at Eucla, driving his T Model Ford or going on the monthly ship. The "road" to the border was only a narrow, rough track. Technically, the mission district also extended north to the border with the Northern Territory and so included the Trans Australia Railway from the eastern end of the Nullarbor Plain to the border with Western Australia.

At some point during his first year, accompanied by BCA's founder S.J. Kirkby, Neville Haviland travelled to the Trans Line to see what could be done for the people in the railway camps. It was a brave venture in a T Model Ford as the "road" north would have literally been camel tracks and they would have had to carry fuel supplies. The trip resulted in giving Kirkby a desire to put a man on the Line, a dream which only became a reality 43 years later.

However, things were to change in the interim!

In 1935, then BCA organising missioner, the Revd Tom Jones [later third Bishop of Willochra], travelled 11,000 miles [17,600 km] through isolated areas of Australia to research places that needed Christian ministry. He wrote in the Society's magazine, *"The Real Australian"* -

> *"I am convinced that there is no portion of the country more in need of help as regards maternity and child welfare, and educational facilities than the Great East-West Railway Line between Port Augusta (South Australia) and Kalgoorlie (Western Australia), a distance of 1000 miles. The need for a medical service on the line is of primary importance."*

In 1937, the BCA built the Bishop Kirkby Memorial Hospital on land provided by Commonwealth Railways at the western end of the township and resident Christian ministry was re-established on the Line. In addition to their medical work, the sisters conducted weekly church services and undertook religious instruction at the school until the hospital closed 61 years later. The Lady Dugan Nursing Hostel [later the Lady Dugan Hospital][26] was opened at Tarcoola in 1940 and a nursing hostel was established at Rawlinna in 1951.

As the result of a specific bequest a year after the hospital opened at Cook, BCA established the Church of England Flying Medical Service. So, with the opening of Bishop Kirkby Memorial Hospital and the establishment of the Church of England Flying Medical Service visits to Cook became more feasible with BCA clergy travelling on the aircraft on a regular basis to take services of Holy Communion.

The Revd Herb Broadley was priest-in-charge during 1935-1940 when the FMS was established and again in 1942-1946. He and Revd John Greenwood [later organising missioner] who was assistant priest in 1944-

45 went to Cook travelling on the aeroplane or by car and may have used the Welfare Car.

Meanwhile, a new mission district, also cut off from Streaky Bay, was created in 1936. Centred on Minnipa, 108 miles east of Ceduna. it included the farming country south to Lock and east to Wudinna and Kyancutta. The Rt Revd Richard Thomas, the second Bishop of Willochra appealed to the Bush Church Aid Society for a clergyman. The Revd Leon Morris, later Principal of Ridley College, with his wife Mildred, offered to take up the appointment and in 1940 he became the priest in charge. He later wrote:

> *"As the bishop added some sheep station country to my parish I asked, 'where will my northern boundary be'? He looked at me in surprise. 'There is no one working north of you', he said, 'Go as far as you can'. The result? A parish area totalling about 40,000 square miles. I had a service for my farmers once a fortnight, while the stations saw me once in three months"*[27].

Leon Morris extended his pastoral ministry north to take in Tarcoola. Travel was up the track from the Eyre Highway to Kingoonya. 50 miles east of Tarcoola. Kingoonya was the point where the 'road' which became the Stuart Highway led north to Alice Springs and Darwin. There were three sheep stations to visit on the way including Lake Everard where the Morris's stayed overnight and he conducted a Communion Service the next morning.

One interesting story of these trips is that Mildred drove most of the time while Leon read and studied for his Master's degree. How anyone could read and make legible notes while bouncing over the rough track seems unbelievable[28].

5.
THE MINISTRY GROWS

At some point in the early 1950s, because of financial problems in the Diocese of Willochra, the archdeaconry of Eyre Peninsula was returned to the Diocese of Adelaide. BCA clergy continued their ministries.

Herb Broadley was succeeded at Ceduna by Revd Philip Connell. He and his wife Gladys had served with BCA at Rappville in the Diocese of Grafton for the previous three years. Knowing Philip Connell's wonderful pastoral heart[29], I am sure he would have visited Cook regularly, perhaps once a month, to encourage the sisters at the hospital and conduct Communion services. He travelled on the BCA aeroplane and may even have done occasional trips by car as fuel supplies in the form of 44 gallon drums could be brought to Cook by rail and secured in a lock-up shed beside the airstrip. He may have travelled on the train to Rawlinna to encourage Sister Edna Thomas and possibly have used the Welfare Car.

In late 1945, when Leon Morris concluded his BCA service, John Greenwood succeeded him and built on the ministry that the Morris's had established. He visited Tarcoola and the sheep stations once a quarter. He celebrated Holy Communion at Tarcoola and at some of the stations. He also took Scripture classes at Tarcoola and Kingoonya to relieve the nursing sisters as well as visiting homes in both "towns". In addition to their medical work, the sisters at Cook and Tarcoola, as well as Edna Thomas at Rawlinna, had vibrant pastoral ministries. Philip Connell and John Greenwood both concluded their ministries in 1950. With the "changing of the guard", Theo Hayman was appointed priest-in-charge of Ceduna and George Fuhrmeister priest-in-charge of Minnipa. It was during their tenures that an exciting new development that would aid their ministry occurred.

For the first sixteen years from the founding of the Church of England Flying Medical Service, emergency communication between the hospitals and Ceduna was the basic Commonwealth Railways and PMG telephone systems via Port Augusta. However, in 1954, a radio base was established at Ceduna with the call sign VKB. This connected the hospitals and sheep stations with the base and each other. All these locations had transceivers with their own call signs. Cook Hospital's was 9RO; Tarcoola Hospital's was 9RP. The Ceduna and Minnipa clergy also had portable transceivers in their vehicles which meant that they could venture further afield by car with confidence as well as keep in touch with the parish centres while they were away. It also meant that it was easier to plan outreach ministry as they could contact the stations beforehand and draw up an itinerary. The Ceduna clergy call sign was 9TH [Theo's initials] and the Minnipa [later, Tarcoola] clergy call sign was 9TG.

Theo Hayman used the *Tea and Sugar* a couple of times a year, probably before Easter and Christmas, to visit the settlements west as far as Rawlinna which meant he could encourage Edna Thomas. 304 miles [486 km] west of Cook, Rawlinna was part of the Diocese of Kalgoorlie. Theo returned to Cook on the Passenger Express or the Fast Goods train. BCA ministry along the Line had been extended.

George Fuhrmeister, who succeeded John Greenwood, visited Tarcoola and Kingoonya four times a year and extended the sheep/cattle station ministry further north to the 30th parallel of latitude, the border between the two dioceses, about 70 miles [110 km] south of the Coober Pedy opal fields. George Fuhrmeister's ministry in Minnipa ended in 1956 when he was transferred to Quorn, a town north-east of Port Augusta. A year later, in 1957, Theo Hayman concluded his ministry at Ceduna and became rector of Marryatville, an Adelaide suburb. He was later to become organising missioner of BCA. Theo Hayman was succeeded at Ceduna by Revd Tom Jones, Jr. The Revd Arthur and Pat Williams who succeeded the Fuhrmeister's at Minnipa continued the ministry at Tarcoola and Kingoonya, visiting at least once a quarter. In 1960, Arthur and Pat moved to Mt Magnet in the Diocese of North West Australia, following an appeal for a clergyman from Bishop John Frewer. Arthur was later appointed NSW Secretary of BCA.

The Revd Bill Warburton followed Arthur Williams at Minnipa. Bill had been missioner at Tarraleah in Tasmania for the previous five years so the move to a hot dry climate was a huge challenge. In contrast to Arthur Williams quiet demeanour, Bill could best be described as ebullient. His enthusiasm knew no bounds. In addition to two Sundays a month that involved a round trip of 250 miles [400 km] with five services at Minnipa and the surrounding communities, Bill went to Kingoonya, Tarcoola and the northern sheep stations 3-4 times a year.

When Tom Jones concluded his ministry at Ceduna in 1962, the Revd Bernard Buckland with his wife Coralie was transferred from Franklin Harbour, another BCA staffed mission district on the east coast of Eyre Peninsula. For Bernard Buckland, apart from his time at Cook and Rawlinna, his first visit to the Trans Line was frustrating. He drove to Cook on a Saturday spending the afternoon and evening with the sisters. He also visited a couple of keen Christian families. The next morning after celebrating Holy Communion, he boarded the *Tea and Sugar* for Rawlinna. The train, which had stabled overnight, left Cook at 10:15am and after an overnight stop at Loongana, arrived at Rawlinna 24 hours later. Bernard was frustrated at the small amount of time he had in each of the eleven settlements, mostly 1-1½ hours, which only allowed him to introduce himself as people collected their groceries, bought their meat from the butcher and did the rest of their business.

At Rawlinna, Bernard spent two nights at the medical hostel and had good fellowship with Edna Thomas. He conducted a Communion Service and took Scripture classes at the primary school. He also visited most of the homes with Sister Thomas who introduced him to everyone. He left Rawlinna on the Wednesday passenger express which departed at 2.30pm arriving at Cook six hours later. He sat in the observation lounge, the rear carriage of the express, and spent much of the journey pondering how ministry along the Line could be improved.

Before leaving Cook, Bernard took Scripture classes at the school and talked with stationmaster Dave Reid, a committed Christian, about how he could spend more time in the settlements on future visits. Dave thought he could perhaps travel to one of the fettler camps by either passenger express or goods train, stay overnight, and then catch another train to a further camp. Dave gave him a copy of the official working timetable and suggested he contact the Chief Traffic Manager's office in Port Augusta.

Back at Ceduna over the next few months, Bernard thought about doing a three-week ministry trip along the Line and discussed this with Port Augusta who said such a trip was possible. So, using the working timetable, he planned an itinerary that would enable him to visit twelve settlements as well as go to Kalgoorlie and meet Bishop Cecil Muschamp in whose diocese half the settlements were located. With travel back and forth on various trains, the entire trip had to be planned in conjunction with the Commonwealth Railways management so that train drop offs and pickups could be authorised. Commonwealth Railways gave him a free pass.

Bernard took a huge amount of equipment which had to be loaded or unloaded at each stop. The equipment included a 12-volt generator weighing a hundredweight [50.8kg], a movie projector, films, a screen, tinned and dried food, boxes of books, magazines and tracts in various languages, a suitcase with clothes. The reading material in different languages was because many of the fettlers were assisted migrants from Europe with limited English. They had to work for the government in remote communities for two years in return for the assistance.

Once at a settlement, Bernard visited each house during the day. After the gang returned, the screen was set up in a shed and the projector placed on a 44-gallon drum outside. The residents sat inside on chairs they brought from their homes. The generator would be started to power the projector and the meeting would start with documentaries followed by a Gospel film and a short talk. The first trip was such a success that a second one was undertaken later in the year when Bernard visited another dozen camps. It was a revolutionary concept and set the pattern for future ministry along the Trans Line.

6.
CHANGE, CHANGE, CHANGE

Ordained in 1961 and after two curacies in Sydney, I began my BCA ministry at the end of February 1963 as assistant priest at Ceduna. Although licensed to Bernard Buckland as curate, I was effectively the third man in Ceduna and Minnipa Mission Districts which meant there would always be a priest "in town" when one was in the "Bush".

Two weeks later, as I was beginning to find my feet in outback South Australia after a year in inner-city Sydney, the world turned upside down or, so it seemed! Assistant organising missioner Bill Rich arrived in Ceduna to pay a pastoral visit to the field staff. After spending a day with the sisters, the doctor, the pilots, the pharmacist and the radio base operator, he met with Bernard and me.

Over morning tea, he told us that Arthur Williams was leaving Mt Magnet and BCA was now looking for a clergyman to replace him. Bernard, who was later to become Assistant Bishop of North West Australia, blurted, "We'll go". Coralie was unhappy with the amount of time he was away on patrols and that was affecting their marriage and his ministry in town. I think Bill was relieved at that response but it stunned me. Bernard now had to decide when he would leave Ceduna and give the bishop a month's notice. As if all this was not enough, Bill Rich told us the Warburtons were leaving Minnipa on a date to be decided because of his son's illness and the need to be in cooler climate. It was hoped that a new missioner for Ceduna could be found quickly so that I could be locum at Minnipa.

A week after Bill Rich's visit, I undertook the scheduled patrol along the Eyre Highway instead of Bernard. After taking the fortnightly Sunday service at Penong [50 miles west of Ceduna], I stayed overnight at the hospital with Sister Vera Holle. The next day, I headed west to Eucla on the track that was called the Eyre Highway, stopping at Koonalda station for lunch. That night, at Eucla, I celebrated Holy Communion with a congregation of seven - the Gurney family and two tourists staying at the roadhouse/motel. There was an hilarious incident before the service. While the Gurney family were getting ready, the bell rang to indicate that a car had arrived and the driver wanted fuel. I went out, fully robed, and served them. They were somewhat startled. I would have loved to be a "fly on the wall" when they arrived at their destination to recount the story.

The following morning, I went on to Mundrabilla, 65 miles west and technically part of the parish of Norseman, where the station owner and his wife were committed Christians. Again, I celebrated Holy Communion and stayed overnight before heading back to Ceduna with a lunch stop at Nullarbor station. By the time I returned, Bernard had planned the next trip along the Trans Line which I would now undertake.

On the Friday after Easter, we packed the panel van and headed west on the Eyre Highway. After 3½ hours we arrived at the turnoff to the railway line which had a sign post, "Cook 100 miles" although as we drove, it seemed further than that. If the Eyre Highway west of Penong was a track, at least it was graded a couple of times a year. The road to Cook was never graded and could best be described as a goat track!

CHANGE, CHANGE, CHANGE

We arrived at Cook mid-afternoon, unloaded the equipment at the railway station and settled into our accommodation at the hospital. We had some great fellowship with Sisters Maud Ross and Marge Tarr. The next morning, Bernard headed back to Ceduna.

On Sunday, after celebrating Holy Communion, I had lunch with Dave and Marg Reid. As we talked over my plans for the next three weeks, Dave gave me the names of all the gangers as well as the senior staff at Rawlinna.

I learned something new about the Trans Line on that first Sunday in Cook. During supper after the evening service in the hospital loungeroom, Dave took me to the western veranda. There was a glow of light in the distant horizon before a bright pinpoint of light appeared. I turned and said, "Crumbs, I better start getting ready to go". He laughed and replied, "It's forty minutes out; there is no hurry. We'll go over to the station when the driver sounds the hooter". That made me realise how vast and flat the Nullarbor Plain is! However, a few nights later the experience had slipped my memory.

I was at Loongana, due to leave early in the morning. The ganger and his wife had kindly offered me a bed. After checking with the train controller how the train was running and setting the alarm, I went to bed early. I woke at 11:30 with a dry throat and went into the kitchen to get a glass of water. Looking out the window, there was a glow in the horizon and without thinking of Cook, I grabbed my clothes, stuffed them into the sleeping bag, quietly opened the door and rushed to the station shed in my pajamas and bare feet, picking up prickles on the way. It was May and a cold night; the winter temperature on the Nullarbor drops below freezing point at night. After I dressed beside the railway line, I sat shivering for two hours until the train finally arrived, late, at 1.30am.

But back to Cook on that Sunday night.

After loading all the equipment into the brake van[30], I boarded the passenger express for Barton, 137 miles [219 km] east of Cook to begin my first patrol to the isolated settlements along the Trans Australia Railway. Nestling in the sandhills of the Great Victoria Desert, Barton was a coaling station and a changeover point in the former steam train days. It had a solidly built crew rest house with several bedrooms, a lounge/dining room and kitchen. The ganger's wife was the housekeeper and the beds were always made up. The train arrived at Barton at 2:00am on a moonlit night. With the guard's help, I unloaded the baggage, leaving everything except my suitcase in the station shed and made my way to the rest house where a light was shining in a bedroom. I went to sleep with a dingo howling

Getting up four hours later, I introduced myself to the gang before they went off to work at 7 o'clock and was warmly welcomed. Before they left, the men carried all my gear to the rest house. After some breakfast, I had an unhurried time with the Lord before spending the morning visiting the wives. Again, I was well received. They were glad to receive the literature, especially those who were non-English speakers, and talk. Following some lunch, I had a rest before getting things ready for early evening meeting.

I set up the screen and the speakers in a shed with the projector outside on a 44-gallon drum, I started the generator and checked that everything was working. When people arrived, a curtain covered the door with just a big enough opening to screen the films. At 5 o'clock the entire population was present. Of course, it was rare entertainment but after the gospel film was screened there was some good conversation.

The ganger and his wife invited me to dinner which was an unexpected pleasure. It allowed time to discuss their personal difficulties and some of the problems within the community. I realised how valuable this ministry would be as relationships developed. Unlike town and city, it was unhurried.

CHANGE, CHANGE, CHANGE

Retracing my tracks, I left for Reid, 120 miles west of Cook, on the Fast Goods around 10 o'clock the next morning arriving just after 6:00pm WA time[31]. The gang was on hand to help me unload the equipment, which was put in the small station shed. It was too late to have a meeting that night but I was delighted to be invited to stay at the ganger's house with opportunity again to discuss problems in the settlement.

The next day I spent a lot of time visiting the homes, drinking cups of tea and talking with the women. Again, people were glad to receive the literature. There was an empty house at Reid so the projector and screen were set up in the loungeroom with the generator outside. Everyone brought chairs to the meeting. I left Reid that night and travelled further west to another settlement. This was to be my life for the next three weeks, travelling back and forth between settlements before finally going to Kalgoorlie for the last two days to stay with Bishop Muschamp and his wife Peggy who were a gracious host and hostess.

The bishop and I established a strong rapport from the outset and in fact I acted as his chaplain at a Confirmation service in the parish of St Matthew's Boulder the first night. That was an experience for a young priest from the Diocese of Sydney! Bishop Cecil was an old-fashioned Anglo-Catholic and there were clouds of incense during the service. As well as taking me on a tour of Kalgoorlie the next day, including a visit to one of the batteries to see a gold pour, the bishop and I spent most of the time discussing ministry. He told me how delighted he was that we had extended the ministry along the Trans Line to include the part that was in his diocese. He was very encouraging.

The following day, I returned to Cook on the passenger express departing Kal at 8:15am. It was a very comfortable 12-hour journey and I spent the time reading, talking with other passengers, some of whom I discovered were BCA supporters. I spent the night at Cook before going back to

Ceduna in the Cessna which had come up for me. I had travelled 3400 [5440 km] miles by train during the three weeks.

Back at Ceduna, Bernard was keen to hear about the trip and was delighted that it had gone so well. He told me I could have Sunday and a couple of days off. During lunch, I learned that the Revd Harry Goodhew was to succeed him and would be instituted at the end of June. I had known Harry, who was later to become Archbishop of Sydney, for several years and had helped him establish a CEBS[33] branch at St Matthew's Bondi during my first year at Moore College. I was both delighted and disappointed at his appointment. Delighted that he was coming; disappointed that I would not be working with him because I was going to Minnipa.

7.
EXPECT THE UNEXPECTED

With Bernard's farewell in a couple of weeks, Bill Warburton planned his final visit to Tarcoola while there were still three clergy. I would look after the Minnipa services that weekend.

I drove to Minnipa on the Thursday to discover that because Margaret was unwell, Bill had decided to stay at home and I would do the trip north. During the evening, Bill and I discussed the itinerary and the people I would meet, The next morning I headed north in the Minnipa car with its portable transceiver. I stayed the night at Lake Everard homestead where Bill and Pat Williams provided great hospitality.

After a Communion service early the next morning, I continued north to Kingoonya, stopping at Kokatha station where again I was made welcome by Vic and Betty Churches. I had a pub lunch at Kingoonya before driving west to Tarcoola traversing a large salt lake on the way. It was great to meet Sisters Vaisey Cochrane and Jean Griffin who, previously, I had only heard about. As there were no patients, we had a relaxed evening.

On the Sunday I had morning and evening services with some of the congregation having travelled in 80 miles [over 125 km] to worship. In the afternoon Vaisey took me around town to meet other people including stationmaster Jeff Bolitho, police sergeant Ray Wandel and the schoolteacher.

On Monday, I took a Scripture class before heading to Kingoonya for another class. Both teachers were very warm. After another pub lunch, I headed down the Kingoonya Track for Minnipa without stopping. Margaret Warburton had recovered which was a relief for Bill.

After dinner, Bill and I discussed the parish and what I could expect from the people in the various centres. He also gave me a book with maps of the locations of the farms which Arthur Williams had drawn. Bill gave me details of the Sunday services. Minnipa and Wudinna had weekly services; Poochera and Wirrulla had monthly services; other centres had services twice a month. The next day it was back to Ceduna

The next couple of weeks were rather hectic. Coralie had already left Ceduna with the children. Bernard spent most of the time packing personal things as well as talking with me about what needed to be done. He left two days after his farewell on the last Sunday in May.

Before I left Sydney, I had become engaged to Jan McDougall, a double certificated nursing sister and student at Deaconess House in Sydney. We planned our wedding for the last week of February 1964. Our ongoing relationship was confined to occasional expensive phone calls and letters which was somewhat frustrating.

Early in May, Jan had run out of money and, rather than go into debt, she decided to leave Deac House and return to nursing. She initially went home to Newcastle to spend time with her mother. Then, before she looked for a nursing placement, my aunt felt that we needed to have time together and paid for her to come to Ceduna for a holiday. In early June, I drove to Adelaide to meet Jan which also enabled me to do some shopping. One of the BCA pilots, John Lindridge and his wife Marie provided Jan with accommodation in Ceduna.

After three weeks, during which we visited many parts of the parish together, including Koonalda station where we picked up a promised puppy, Jan decided to stay and nurse with the Society. Matron Florence Dowling mulled over where to send her and finally in her own gruff way said to her, "I have vacancies at Penong and Wudinna; while I would like to fill Penong, I will send you to Wudinna and we might get some work out of both of you". Wudinna is only 24 miles from Minnipa.

Harry and Pam Goodhew arrived with their family in late June. During the week before Harry's induction on the last Friday that month, I filled him in on the bush region of the parish - the Eyre Highway and the Trans Line. The day after his institution, I drove to Minnipa. Margaret Warburton had already left for Tasmania with the children. Bill and I did the Sunday ministry together before he left on the following Tuesday.

I was on my own!

I settled into work in the parish. That included the two Sundays with a round trip of 250 miles and services at Minnipa [8.00am], Lock [10.30am], Warrimoo [2.00pm], Kyancutta [3.30pm], Wudinna [7.00pm]. I had lunch at the golf club as the guest of different families at Lock. There was a room off the veranda at Wudinna Hospital for the missioner and so, after the service and supper, I stayed overnight as Jan and I both had Mondays free and could spend time together. We explored the district and had picnics as far north as Yardea station, 30 miles up the Kingoonya Track.

But just as I was establishing a routine, once again, came the unexpected!

In the first week of August, I received a phone call from Bill Rich with the news that the Bishop of Adelaide had advised the Society that he wanted to excise the station country north and south of the Trans Line and appoint a diocesan priest to a smaller Minnipa Mission District. Bishop Reed suggested that he could create a new mission district based at Tarcoola or Cook to include the sheep stations and the South Australian section of the Trans

Line. The bishop asked if BCA would provide a priest. Bill invited me to take up the appointment.

After praying about this, Jan and I agreed to accept the appointment providing we could bring our marriage forward before moving to Tarcoola. Both the bishop and the Society were comfortable with this so Jan returned home to prepare for our wedding which was now set for 9 November. I made a Tarcoola/sheep station visit in mid- September and drove back east a month later. After our wedding at All Saints' Balgowlah and a honeymoon at Gerringong on the NSW South Coast, we returned to Minnipa to begin our life together.

Apart from routine parish work in December, we went up to Tarcoola for a weekend before Christmas. Then, with many farmers away, January was a quiet month during which I began to wind up BCA's ministry at Minnipa in preparation for our move. This involved sorting out what belonged to the parish and what belonged to the Bush Church Aid Society. The furniture was BCA's and would go to Tarcoola.

Meanwhile, Jan had fallen pregnant and was suffering from high blood pressure. Dr Douglas would only allow her to go to Tarcoola providing she went on the BCA aircraft and stayed a few days in the hospital after her arrival.

In early February 1964, I drove to Adelaide where I took delivery of a custom-built Land Rover. Although a basic vehicle, it had two 20 gallon [91 litres] fuel tanks, racks for two 4-gallon jerry cans, a 20-gallon water tank and two spare wheels – one on the bonnet, the other inside the rear compartment. Staying overnight in Adelaide with cousins, I read the owner's manual, practiced with the four-wheel-drive transfer box up and down the street, my only training, before I headed back to Minnipa.

A couple of days later, I drove Jan to Wudinna hospital where she would stay before she was flown to Tarcoola, I then headed up the Kingoonya

Track with a stop at Lake Everard. The truck with the furniture and personal effects came up a couple of days later.

BCA leased one of the two large PMG houses at the eastern end of town, only one of which was occupied by the department. The railway line was less than 100 metres from the front fence on the other side of Tarcoola Parade. There was nothing but saltbush and the remains of the goldmining town beyond the back fence apart from the taxiway which led from the airstrip to the hospital.

The house had a large lounge room off which there was the kitchen and three bedrooms, one of which would be a study. A wide enclosed veranda wrapped around two thirds of the house. Commonwealth Railways supplied water to us at the same rate their staff enjoyed; 4/- [40c] per 1000 gallons as opposed to 16/6 [$1.65] that the Police Department, Education Department, the PMG and the hotel paid. They also provided free electricity to us and the hospital.

My first year in the "Bush" was over during which I had travelled 42,000 miles [67,000km] by road as well as the 3400 miles by rail. It was time for the new venture.

8.
THE 1000 MILE LONG PARISH

I was instituted as priest in charge of Tarcoola by Archdeacon of Eyre Peninsula Malcolm Gooden on Friday 14 February. The church was full for the occasion. The congregation included stationmaster Jeff Bolitho, the BCA's sisters, the schoolteacher, the police sergeant's family, some railway workers with their families and a couple of sheep station families.

The archdeacon preached from Ezekiel 33:1-9 with verse 7 as his text – *"Son of man, I have made you a watchman for the house of Israel; so hear the word I speak and give them warning from me"*. That sermon and verse largely shaped my entire future ministry.

I was now the minister of a "parish" that in theory extended along the railway line from Port Augusta to the Western Australian border. However, in practice, I only regularly ministered east as far as Condambo, with occasional visits to Pimba. The priest-in-charge of Woomera, 4 miles north of Pimba ministered to the surrounding settlements from time to time; the Port Augusta clergy ministered north halfway to Pimba. In effect, however, the "parish" extended to the western end of the Line when the Bishop of Kalgoorlie gave me his "Authority to Officiate".

THE 1000 MILE LONG PARISH

With tongue in cheek, I used to claim it was the only 'parish' in the world that was 1000 miles long and 4 feet 8½ inches wide. South of Tarcoola and Kingoonya with the sheep/cattle stations, it extended to within 30 miles of the Eyre Highway and 260 miles [416km] north up the old Stuart Highway. It also included the huge sheep stations north-west of Tarcoola. It was a total area of 85,000 square miles [over 220,000 square kilometres]

Having described the Tarcoola Mission district, I now want to concentrate on the ministry along the Trans Australia Railway during which I travelled 29,000 miles [46,400 km] by train and over 36,000 miles [57,600 km] by road between February 1964 and May1966. I used to joke that I spent half my life with "a Land Rover strapped to the seat of my pants."

The first thing Jan and I had to learn was that life at Tarcoola would be largely governed by the arrival and departure of trains. I had to develop a good relationship with the management in Port Augusta, especially the train controllers as well as with stationmaster Jeff Bolitho who was effectively the "mayor" of Tarcoola. I also had to consider how I would minister along the Line and how regularly.

As mentioned in the first chapter, steam locomotives had been replaced by diesel electric locomotives which did not require supplies of coal and water. Refueling only took place at Cook, as did topping up water for the express carriages. Crews began/ended their shifts at Port Augusta where most of them lived, at Tarcoola, Cook, Rawlinna and Parkeston/Kalgoorlie. There was a passenger express six days a week with westbound trains arriving at Tarcoola at 12:30am and eastbound at 4:30am. There were Fast (express) Goods trains every day. The westbound arrived at 7:00am or thereabouts; the eastbound around 5:30pm. As well as these trains, there were smaller additional Special Goods several days a week as well as the weekly Slow Mixed Goods train [*the Tea and Sugar*].

As previously mentioned, the *Tea and Sugar* left Port Augusta at 6:00am every Thursday. It made an overnight stop at Pimba before arriving at Tarcoola around 11.00am/midday on Friday. Its arrival heralded the busiest two hours of the week with a lot of shunting of wagons. It was very much a social occasion. Although we could buy basic groceries at the general store, Jan had to learn to buy meat for the week from the butcher's van. In addition to this, we eventually arranged for a box of fresh fruit and vegetables to be sent up from the Adelaide Markets once a fortnight.

The BCA sisters were highly respected and had good relationships in town but realising I was a bit of a novelty, I spent the first couple of weeks wandering around town greeting people to introduce myself. They were friendly, although somewhat wary of having a clergyman living in town. I conducted services on the first two Sundays, Holy Communion in the morning and an evening service. They were reasonably well attended. I also visited Kingoonya to teach Scripture in the school and have a lunchtime service in the hotel. That was to become a fortnightly visit.

I travelled to Cook on the Friday morning passenger train for the third weekend of each month arriving at 8:00am with accommodation at the hospital. I took Scripture classes that morning and spent much of the day talking with Dave Reid. I spent Saturday walking around town to meet people and introducing myself to those I had not previous met. There were two Sunday services, Holy Communion in the morning and Evening Prayer. I caught the express back to Tarcoola on Sunday night. That was to become the routine for the third weekend every month.

After this introduction to the ministry, it was time to think ahead. With Easter approaching. I made plans for the Welfare Car to be attached to the *Tea and Sugar* so Jan and I could make a trip west to Kalgoorlie together, visit every camp and conduct a service at the settlements where the train stabled overnight.

On the Friday before Palm Sunday, Jan and I with our dog *Snoopy* boarded the Welfare Car when the T*ea and Sugar* arrived at Tarcoola and headed west for an overnight stop at Barton. The following nights were spent at Cook, Haig and Rawlinna where I conducted a Communion service at the BCA nursing hostel. The next two days saw us go to Zanthus and on to Parkeston where the carriage was shunted onto a siding. We spent a day in Kalgoorlie with the bishop and the next day the Welfare Car was attached to the Fast Goods which took us to Cook. Again, the carriage was shunted to a siding so I could take a Good Friday service. That evening, we were attached to the Fast Goods for the overnight run to Tarcoola in time for me to conduct the Easter services. After that first Easter, I undertook a trip to the northern sheep/cattle stations on my own as we deemed it unwise for Jan to travel over the rough roads.

Jan returned to NSW in early May for her brother David's wedding. I was unable to go because I had used up all my leave entitlement for our wedding the previous November. I drove Jan to Adelaide to catch the plane to Sydney. Back home, with Jan away, I decided that it was time for the next venture, a Land Rover patrol along the Line to Kalgoorlie with overnight stops at every third settlement.

9.
DEVELOPING THE MINISTRY

After that beginning, in addition to the third Sunday at Cook, I planned to conduct services at Tarcoola on the other three Sundays each month although this plan had to be amended as will be seen later. The BCA nurses would take the services at Tarcoola and Cook on the other Sundays as they had done for many years. Planning for ministry along the Line and visits to the sheep/cattle stations had to be drawn up. There were sixteen sheep/cattle stations to visit. Commonwealth Hill [4600 square miles with 60,000 sheep] and Mulgathing were north west of Tarcoola; Wilgena and Bulgunnia were east of Tarcoola. North Well, Bon Bon, Mt Eba, Millers Creek, Billa Kalina, McDouall Peak and Ingomar were north of Kingoonya off the Stuart Highway. Kokatha, Lake Everard, Thurlga and Yardea were south on the Kingoonya Track.

I decided to do three patrols along the Line in the Land Rover each year. This would enable me to have extended time in every settlement, staying overnight at each settlement once a year. It also allowed me to stop and spend time with the fettlers beside the track where they were working. It was rewarding both for my "parishioners" and me as we got to know one another and I gained their confidence.

DEVELOPING THE MINISTRY

With Jan away, I undertook my first patrol along the Trans Line. As I loaded the Land Rover with everything I needed – clothing, movie projector, screen, generator, books, magazines, tinned and dry food, first aid kit, my camera and the transceiver to keep me connected with Ceduna and Tarcoola, as well as food for *Snoopy* who would go with me, little did I know what was in store.

Before I left, Ray Wandel, the police officer, told me he had driven to Cook once and would never do it again. Ah well, I had made plans, everyone knew I was coming and I had organised 44-gallon drums of fuel at Cook and Rawlinna. I topped up the fuel and water tanks, filled the jerry cans and off I went, with a stop to talk with the Wynbring gang near Malbooma [the siding for Commonwealth Hill sheep station], before spending an hour or so at Wynbring. Going on, I soon reached the Dog Fence. I had to open the gate to pass through and then close it.

The Dog Fence is designed to keep dingoes[34] out of the south-east part of the continent and protect the sheep flocks of South Australia and southern Queensland. One of the longest structures in the world, it is 3,488 miles [5,614 km] long and stretches from the Great Australian Bight near Nundroo [97 miles west of Ceduna] to the Darling Downs near Dalby passing through Coopers Corner, where the borders of NSW, The Northern Territory and Queensland meet. Contractors each patrol a 200 mile stretch weekly and make repairs where necessary.

Not long after passing through the Dog Fence I was into the sandhills of the Great Victoria Desert heading for Barton. Although sand, the track at his stage was easy to negotiate. On the way, I had a cup of tea with the single men's gang from Mount Christie. Barton was my first overnight stop and I had a bed at the rest house. When I arrived, the gang was back and I chatted with some of them as I set up the projector for an evening meeting. I had dinner that night with the ganger and his wife. Before dinner, I visited the four out of six houses that were occupied. We had a good evening meeting with a couple of documentaries and a Christian film. There were several questions and I was able to share my testimony. Like everybody else, although I had only driven about 120 miles [190 km], I was ready for bed at 9 o'clock.

The next morning, I set off early for what was to be a challenge. I was in the lower bulge of the Great Victoria Desert and had to negotiate sandhills for the 50-mile run to Ooldea. It was my first experience of real four-wheel-driving and involved climbing and descending the sandhills, some of which were 60 feet or more high. The track was close to the railway line which was comforting. On the way I stopped for a cup of tea and yarn with a special gang who were doing major reconstruction. They were housed at a temporary camp called Immarna. It consisted of sleeping carriages, a kitchen van with a cook and a dining van, all on a spur line. I was to develop a good relationship with this gang over the next couple of years

After attacking the first sandhill and stalling about a third of the way up, I half slid back to the bottom and realised, as the Owner's Manual suggested, that I would have to lower the tyre pressure. That meant dropping it to 10 pounds per square inch. That done, I successfully climbed the first sandhill, went down the other side into a trough and then began the process again. It was slow going and the last 18 miles [29km] took over 4½ hours as the sand was very loose.

It was a relief to clear the sandhills and arrive at the eastern edge of the Nullarbor Plain ten miles from Ooldea and onto a firm road. However, the ordeal was not yet over. I had to hand pump the tyres back to 28lb psi and that took another hour. When I reached Kalgoorlie at the end of the patrol and visited the Land Rover agent, I discovered that a pump which worked off the engine compression was available. An interesting item of equipment, it involved removing a spark plug, screwing the end of the hose into the empty hole and letting the engine do the hard work. I bought one immediately and was delighted with it on my next trip.

I reached Ooldea camp just after 12:30pm and was welcomed warmly by the ganger's wife who offered me lunch. After the meal and conversation with her, I then visited the other three occupied houses, talked with the women, and left some literature before heading to Watson, twenty miles away, where I would stay the night. Just beyond Ooldea is the last bend in the railway line for nearly 300 miles [475km] – the *Long Straight*.

A few miles west of Ooldea, I came across the gang at work and pulled up. I was greeted by the ganger, who I had met on my first rail trip while at Ceduna. He called the train controller at Port Augusta and said, "George, the padre has arrived and we're going to knock off for a brew"[35]. So, I sat on the edge of the railway line and had a cup of tea with the four guys, something that I could not have done without the Land Rover. It was a wonderful time of questions and answers, something that was to be repeated with other gangs for the entire trip and subsequent patrols.

I arrived at Watson in the late afternoon just as the gang returned from work and was given a great welcome by Kevin, the ganger, who insisted I stay with him and his wife. Watson was a larger settlement than many as it was the railhead for Maralinga, the Atomic Weapons Research Establishment, where major British nuclear and other tests took place between 1953 and 1963. While a bitumen road led 26 miles [42 km] north to Maralinga Village, the headquarters, Maralinga was off limits to civilians. Unbeknown to me at the time, plans were afoot, with BCA approval, for me to fill a CMF[36] vacancy and become part time chaplain at Maralinga which was still a sizeable military base.

After the night at Watson with a similar programme to that at Barton, I headed for Cook, 66 miles [106 km] away, for the weekend arriving in time to take Scripture classes at the school. I spent three days at Cook which allowed for extended home visits, time with the fettlers, train crews, other railway maintenance personnel, Sunday services and a rest day on the Tuesday.

Leaving Cook, the routine over the next couple of weeks was like that of the first few days of the patrol. I visited the women in the settlements, talked with the gangs on the side of the track and stopped overnight at every third camp for meetings. After crossing the South Australia/Western Australia border, I spent the first night at Forrest, travelling only 140 miles (220 km). Forrest was a fully operational airport which had been a refueling, and often an overnight stop, for airlines in the 1940s/1950s when Douglas DC-3 aircraft provided air travel between Sydney/Melbourne and Perth[37]. It is still used by light aircraft and the RAAF[38]. It is also a weather station.

I stayed in the airport accommodation at Forrest with the usual meeting at the railway settlement in the evening and a service of Holy Communion at the aerodrome in the morning as Jim and Margaret Sweeney, the managers, were committed Christians. Some of the people from the railway settlement came over as well.

The next day, I travelled only 166 miles as I visited not only the settlement at Loongana but also the nearby quarry where ballast was being extracted for the railway line. I stopped for the night at 757 Mile camp where a spur line had been constructed on which a small "train" of five carriages was parked. Like Immarna, this included a kitchen/dining car and was the home of a Special Gang involved in reconstruction. I had accommodation and dinner with them and again was to have a special relationship with these men over the years. The Long Straight ends ten miles east of 757 Mile camp at Nurina, a single men's camp, with the first bend in the railway line after Ooldea

DEVELOPING THE MINISTRY

The next day was again only a short run of 60 miles to Rawlinna where I stayed at the BCA nursing hostel with Sister Edna Thomas. Edna was an amazing lady who spent 17 years on her own in the town. She had the largest Sunday School along the Line and effectively "ran" the town. At Rawlinna school I took a Scripture class, had the usual evening meeting, visited the homes and had two services on the Sunday which were well attended.

Leaving the Land Rover at Rawlinna. *Snoopy* and I returned to Tarcoola on the Fast Goods leaving at 2.00pm [3.30pm SA Time] arriving at 7 o'clock the next morning. I spent the day checking mail, writing letters and cleaning the house before having dinner at the hospital. In the mail there were letters from Canon Alan Begbie, rector of Manly NSW and from Bill Rich. Alan, who I had known since my teenage years, was Chaplain-General of the Australian Army. His letter invited me to accept appointment as CMF chaplain at Maralinga. Bill's letter told me that BCA had approved the appointment. I wrote to Alan and accepted the invitation

Leaving *Snoopy* with the sisters, I walked across to the station and checked on the progress of the Express. It was running late so I returned to the house and set the alarm for 4.00am. The express arrived at 5 o'clock and I was on my way to Port Pirie where I connected with an Adelaide train. I checked in at the Grosvenor Hotel opposite Adelaide Station before catching a taxi to the airport to meet Jan and her younger brother Graeme. We spent the night at the Grosvenor before boarding the train for Port Pirie and the Trans Express. On arrival at Tarcoola at 12:30am, Vaisey Cochrane was there with *Snoopy* to meet the train. She walked Jan and Graeme to the 'rectory' while I went on to Rawlinna to complete the rest of the patrol.

I headed for Zanthus, 170 miles away, making a couple of stops to talk with the fettlers and visit the houses at Kitchener, I also stopped at 913 Mile siding where a very enterprising migrant, Toni Zavala, had established lime kilns after completing his two-year contract with Commonwealth Railways. Lime was needed for processing gold ore.

After the night at the Zanthus where I stayed in the crew rest house and had the usual meeting, I drove 62 miles [100 km] north to Cundeelee operated by the Australian Aboriginal Evangelical Mission where I took a school class, had a meeting and great fellowship. I spent the night at Cundeelee before retracing my tracks to Zanthus and heading west to Kalgoorlie on the last 120-mile leg of the patrol. The countryside along this stretch was vastly different to the Nullarbor Plain with masses of bronze eucalypts lining the road. I stopped on the way to talk with the Coonana and Karonie gangs before visiting the homes at each of the two settlements.

On arrival at Parkeston, I stopped at the station office to confirm that a flattop wagon would be ready to transport the Land Rover back to Tarcoola before going to stay with the bishop. The Land Rover had been deemed an item of equipment and with a freight rate of 25%, the cost of transport was £7/8/4 [$14.83], the price of a 44-gallon drum of fuel which I would have used on the return trip by road via Norseman, Eucla and Ceduna. It meant no wear and tear for me or the Landrover. It was, of course, quicker.

Bishop Cecil and Peggy Muschamp welcomed me warmly. The bishop wanted a report on the trip and we chatted over a cup of tea. I spent the night with them and was able to do some shopping the next morning before driving to Parkeston and loading the Landrover.

I spent time talking with the railway employees while the train was made up with the Landrover immediately behind the locomotives to allow for easy shunting at Tarcoola. I then joined truck drivers, whose vehicles were being "piggybacked" to Port Pirie, in one of the carriages at the rear of the train where I would spend the trip. The old carriages had separate compartments where each man had a bed, a shower cubicle and a kitchen/dining area.

DEVELOPING THE MINISTRY

The 2000 feet [615 metres] long train pulled out of Parkeston slowly at 3:00pm as the slack between the wagons was taken up. The train made scheduled stops at Rawlinna and Cook as well as stops at crossing loops to allow other trains to pass. After a 26-hour trip I arrived at Tarcoola at 5:30pm the next evening The wagon with the Landrover was shunted on to a siding where I left it overnight. This patrol set a pattern for the rest of our time at Tarcoola.

It was wonderful to be home with Jan and to relax for the last few days of May and early June. After all, there was a limit to how many home visits I could make in a town of 27 houses. I visited the two sheep stations northwest of Tarcoola and made a first weekend visit to Maralinga about which I will say more later.

10.

SEPARATION, A DILEMMA AND JOY

Towards the end June, it was time for Graeme to return home. I drove him to Adelaide which gave me the opportunity to purchase a supply of Christian books and magazines.

Near Port Pirie, I stopped to make a planned radio call to Tarcoola where BCA doctor Merna Meuller was on her scheduled monthly visit, I wanted to get her report on the pregnancy with the baby due towards the end of August. Merna told me that Jan's blood pressure was abnormally high and she wanted to take her back to Ceduna on the plane so she could monitor her condition daily and have her near the bigger hospital. I then spoke with Jan and said I thought she should accept Merna's advice even though we would be separated for two months.

By this time, Jan's older brother David, and his wife Anne, had arrived in Ceduna where he was to operate the radio base, which meant Jan could at least be with family. Also, Anne was a registered nurse and midwife. Despite what would be hard for both of us, I could talk with Jan on the radio each day.

I was rather subdued for the rest of the trip to Adelaide and was glad to drop Graeme at the airport for his flight to Sydney. I drove to North

Adelaide and spent the night with my cousins Bob and Mary Wyndham[39]. The next day, I headed back to Port Augusta where I stayed with Bev and Betty Jennings. Bev, a train driver, often called in on us at Tarcoola when his shift ended. As I left Port Augusta the next day, I was tempted to drive to Ceduna but I went on to Tarcoola. I then had to plan the next couple of months.

In the second week of July, I visited the sheep stations to the south stopping at Kingoonya to take a school class. As Yardea station took me to within 100 miles of Ceduna, I went on to spend a couple of days with Jan. When I returned to Tarcoola I decided to do the next Landrover patrol along the Line early. The baby was due on 25 August, so at the end of the trip I could drive from Kalgoorlie to Ceduna via Norseman and be there when the baby arrived.

Well, that was the plan!

I began the second patrol along the Line with *Snoopy* as my companion and had a first overnight stop at Mount Christie single men's camp. From there, I had an hour at Barton before attacking the sandhills once again. I had a cup of tea with the Immarna gang and once on the flat ground, I tried out my new compression pump. It was fantastic and all four tyres were pumped up in about 15 minutes. I drove on to Watson but did not stop there and went north to Maralinga where I spent the weekend. It was a good visit as I was able to meet with the personnel, chat with the officers at the mess in the evening and go out to the test area with the range engineer, a British Army major. On future patrols I spent 3-4 days at Maralinga.

After the weekend, I returned to Watson and visited the houses before heading to Cook for the night. I took a school class on arrival and had a mid-week service of Holy Communion. From Cook, I drove to Hughes, 30 miles east of the border, where I had a meeting and spent the night before going on to Loongana where I left Landrover for the weekend. *Snoopy* and

I returned to Tarcoola on the passenger express so I could take Sunday services. I spent most of the trip in the guard's van where there were a couple of beds, although went to the dining car for dinner.

On the Monday, before lunch at the hospital, I joined the girls in the radio room for the midday schedule. At the end of the usual opening of the session, David said, "I have traffic for 9RP Tarcoola and 9TG Portable; standing by for medical or emergency calls". Vaisey waited to see if there any emergencies elsewhere before she switched to transmit and said, "John is here with us". David responded, "Jan wants to talk with you at the end of the session".

When Jan came on, it was to tell me, "Darling, I think I'm going into labour". There was a gasp from David, who blurted "I'll keep in touch with you at each session". I talked with Jan at the end of the 5 o'clock session and she had no further news. Before ending the session, David said, "I'll have a special sked with you at 9:00pm". It was the beginning of an anxious night, with the Land Rover 400 miles [640 km] away at Loongana and no other way of getting to Ceduna. The only private car in town belonged to the schoolteacher and had no brakes

At the 9 o'clock radio session, David told me that he and Anne had taken Jan to the hospital an hour earlier. That was the end of the carefully made plans. I stayed in the hospital lounge room until midnight when *Snoopy* and I went across to the railway station to wait for the passenger train. When it reached Cook just before 8:00am, I jumped off the train, shouted at Dave Reid, "Don't let it go before I get back. I'm going across to the hospital to see if Jan has had the baby". I ran across, said hello to the girls, went straight to the radio room and switched on in time to hear David say, "I have traffic for 9RO Cook and 9TG Portable." I switched to transmit and said, "9RO Cook". David responded, "Congratulations

SEPARATION, A DILEMMA AND JOY

Daddy, Michael John was born at 6:30. They are both well". Michael had arrived two weeks early.

Back on the train, the drama was not yet over. When I reached Loongana around 11 o'clock I went to the ganger's house and had a cup of tea with his wife. It was then time to head south, but which track? There were three. I said to Marcia, "Which track goes south to Madura?" to which she responded, "I haven't got clue!" so I said to her, "I'll take the middle track and if a call comes through that I'm in trouble, the guys will know which way to go when they come home". No GPS in those days!

It was 106 miles [170 km] to the Eyre Highway and although the track was in good condition it took nearly three hours to get to Madura roadhouse where I had a cup of coffee, refueled and set off for Ceduna. The road down Madura Pass to the Roe Plain was sealed but then it was dirt until the sealed Eucla Pass.

It was 181 miles to Eucla roadhouse and halfway along this stretch I went into the deepest bulldust hole[40] that I had ever encountered, hitting the rocky edge hard as I came out of it. Stopping at Eucla, I found that the rim of the left-hand front wheel was folded back. Roy Gurney changed the wheel while I had a cup of tea with Margaret before heading off on the final 322 miles [515 km] to Ceduna. East of the border, I stopped at Koonalda sheep station and had dinner with Cyril, Audrey and the Gurney children as the sun set. It was dark when I left with 277 miles [440 km] to go. I arrived at Ceduna at 2:30am, 26 hours after leaving Tarcoola. This epic journey to see my firstborn son had covered a total of 1008 miles [1613 kilometres] by rail and road!

Before going to David and Anne's home, I stopped at the hospital on the edge of town and rang the night bell. Sister Elaine Dearden, with whom I had been involved in youth ministry in Sydney, was on duty. She opened the door and, pointing to the first room said, "Jan is in there. Do you want to see the baby? I'll go and get him". She returned and handed Michael to me. As I gazed at him, Elaine said, "You have got a beaut suntan." I looked at her, ran my finger across my forehead and said "Suntan? It's dust". Elaine grabbed the baby and took him back to the nursery.

I spent three days in Ceduna, which gave me some quality time with Jan and Michael John. Because he was a premmie baby, Dr Meuller wanted to keep him at the hospital for the week and fly them to Tarcoola when she went up for her monthly surgery six days later. Sister Dowling gave Jan a room in the nurses' quarters. I stayed with David and Anne. I also spent an evening with Harry Goodhew, sounding him out on the possibility of using the BCA holiday shack at Smoky Bay for a children's camp in January. Harry was very positive about that and we drew up tentative plans for a week-long camp.

I left on the 260-mile (416 km) journey to Tarcoola via Wirrulla and the Kingoonya Track on Friday morning, stopping overnight at Lake Everard station with a service of Holy Communion in the early morning. As usual, Pat and Bill Williams invited the overseers and their families from the outstations to join the service at 6:30. Two couples had an hour's drive. I stopped at Kokatha to have morning tea with Vic and Betty Churches and reached Tarcoola mid-afternoon.

Sunday morning was joyful with everyone full of congratulations and wanting to hear about the baby. When Jan and Michael arrived from Ceduna they spent a couple of days at the hospital before coming home. We set up a nursery in a part of enclosed veranda which had doors from our bedroom and the kitchen.

During the next few months, I spent most days in Tarcoola, visiting, studying and doing some forward planning, I did a short overnight trip to nearby sheep stations. With both of us home we started a mid-week Bible study which was attended by half a dozen members of the congregation.

SEPARATION, A DILEMMA AND JOY

A couple of weeks after Jan returned home, I drove across to the railway station to pick up a parcel. On the way across the railway compound, I stopped to say hello to Jeff Bolitho, who ignored me and walked away. I had developed a good relationship with him and said, "Jeff, what's wrong?" He replied. "Can I come and see you when I finish the shift"? I suggested 2:30 and he responded "I'll see you then". That afternoon, he confessed that while drunk he had punched his wife who now had a black eye. He said, "I've asked God and Pat to forgive me. Is there any hope of me becoming a Christian?" I shared John 3:16 with him and then led him to the Lord which had a dramatic effect on both his personal life and the town.

When Lutheran pastor Heine Noack heard all the news, he wrote, *It reminds me of Alexander the Great, who on the day he received news that his first son was born, conquered a city.* Jeff's conversion was rather like that. In a sense it was a testimony to Heine's ministry as he and others sowed the seed; I had the privilege of harvesting the crop.

11.
THE REST OF THAT FIRST YEAR

There were a lot of changes to the hospital staff during the year. Marge Tarr came from Cook to Tarcoola to replace Vaisey Cochrane who had been posted to the new cottage hospital at Coober Pedy; Barbara Fox was transferred from Wudinna to Cook.

Planning the children's camp was quite time-consuming. It first required setting dates before contacting Cook, Hughes, Rawlinna and Zanthus to try and establish how many kids might come. Then there were negotiations with Commonwealth Railways to arrange to have at least one carriage attached to a Fast Goods train which would make stops to pick up campers and take them to a selected siding where road transport would take them to Smoky Bay as well as take them back after the camp. Harry Goodhew contacted the bus company in Ceduna to establish a pickup point. The manager of the company suggested Ooldea which had a reasonable track from the Eyre Highway and offered to cover the cost. That meant further negotiation with Commonwealth Railways to finalise plans. I also needed to find staff for the camp.

Towards the end of the year. we published a parish magazine which we named the *Trans Line Ambassador*. Copies were sent on the Tea and Sugar

THE REST OF THAT FIRST YEAR

to the stationmasters and gangers for distribution to every employee along the railway line. It was also sent to all the sheep/cattle stations. It was published every three months after that.

At the end of November, Jan and I with Michael and *Snoopy* set off on a pre-Christmas trip in the Welfare Car, arriving at Parkeston on the first day of December. It was a fun trip in many ways as everybody, especially the children, wanted to see the baby. One special memory is when we arrived at 757 Mile single men's camp. Jan remained on the train and Paddy, the ganger, came on board with two of his team. They were rather awkward and suddenly produced some home-made baby clothes which they had bought at the Provisions' Van. Paddy blurted out, "These are for the little bloke, Missus". They had a look at Michael and then scuttled off the train. It was a precious encounter. During the trip, we also collected the registration fees of £5 [$10] for the children coming to Smoky Bay. At Kalgoorlie, Cecil and Peggy Muschamp gave us a wonderful welcome. We stayed overnight with them before boarding the stabled Welfare Car the next afternoon. Peggy looked after Michael while we did some Christmas shopping.

Returning to Tarcoola attached to the Fast Goods we made two overnight stops – at Rawlinna and Forrest where I held services of Holy Communion. We did not stay at Cook as I was coming there just before Christmas. Two things stick in my mind on that return trip. One, was how hot it was with no air conditioning, only fans. We placed Michael in the wash basin in cold water on several occasions to keep him cool. The other incident was the train racing ahead to avoid a dust storm coming from the north which eventually passed behind us.

Back at Tarcoola on the Saturday, there was quite a shock in the mail which had arrived while we were away. BCA was very much a "faith' ministry in the 1960s and there was a letter advising us that no funds were available for November stipends[41]. It was going to be a lean month foodwise. With the sisters, we prayed for the Lord's provision.

On the Sunday afternoon I took the final Confirmation class in preparation for the bishop's visit the following weekend and headed off for the north station country on the Monday afternoon so I could take pre-Christmas services. My first port of call was Bon Bon station where I stayed overnight. The next morning, before I left, the station manager and his wife, who were going to Adelaide for Christmas, gave me a box containing four dozen eggs. They were placed very carefully in the Land Rover so that the box would not move.

I went on to Ingomar for a service and lunch. Retracing my route, I stopped at McDouall Peak for a service and afternoon tea before travelling through Millers Creek station to Billa Kalina where I stayed the night. Colin Greenfield and his wife Sue were committed Christians, great hosts and very generous. We had some wonderful fellowship after a dinner of roast beef from a yearling steer that had been slaughtered two days earlier.

I celebrated Communion before breakfast the next morning. The meal over, Colin told me to go over to the bowser and refuel the Land Rover as he always did, and added, "Then come to the meat shack". When I got there, Colin was busy putting cuts of beef into a calico bag. There was about 10 pounds [4.5 kg] of sliced fillet, the same amount of sliced rump, a large piece of rump and some bones for *Snoopy*. Colin loaded the bag into the Land Rover beside the box of eggs.

As I said goodbye to them, Sue said that she would call Millers Creek and let them know I was on the way. Millers Creek sheep station was managed by their son-in-law. After a service there and morning tea I was given another calico bag together with a container of 5 gallons [nearly 30 litres] of fresh milk and another with 2 pints [1.3 litres] of cream. The bag contained a side of lamb, another shoulder and loin chops. None of these station people knew of our salary problem. The Lord had answered our prayers and provided abundantly![42]

Heading back to Tarcoola, I stopped at North Well outstation for a Communion service and lunch before arriving home around 3 o'clock. We had great fun packing the freezer and sharing the bounty with the sisters as well as with a few members of the congregation.

On the Friday, I drove the 155 miles [248 km] to Woomera to get Assistant Bishop of Adelaide Donald Redding who had taken a Confirmation service at St Barbara's the previous evening. On the trip back to Tarcoola we collected a harvest of Sturt's Desert Peas to decorate the church. (There was no restriction on picking wildflowers in the far north west in those days).

The bishop had a rest day on the Saturday, although he did visit the hospital. Jan and some of the ladies decorated the church in the afternoon. On Sunday morning, I celebrated Holy Communion and the bishop preached. That afternoon, we had the first Confirmation service ever held at Tarcoola with twelve candidates from the town and a surrounding sheep station. It was a wonderful celebration.

12.

THE MINISTRY AT MARALINGA

The Maralinga Prohibited Area of about 1,300 sq miles [3,300 sq km], replaced Emu Field, 125 miles [200 km] to the north after the first nuclear weapons test in 1953 as Emu was deemed too remote for easy transport access. The choice of Maralinga as the Atomic Weapons Research Establishment required moving the entire Tjarutja tribe who were settled at Yalata south of Ooldea.

Maralinga was a joint project of the Australian and United Kingdom governments, The site was selected by Len Beadell, described as the *Last Australian Explorer*. Len also selected and surveyed the site for Woomera, the Long Range Weapons Establishment. He and his team are best known for building thousands of miles of roads across Central Australia including the famous Gunbarrel Highway.

Maralinga Village, the headquarters of the AWRE, was located 26 miles north of Watson. The test site was 26 miles further to the north east. A bitumen road was constructed from Watson to the *village* and another to the test area. The *village* was a typical military base with a headquarters area, barracks, officers, sergeants and general messes. There was a vehicle maintenance facility and everything else that a military base needs. In addition, there were electricity generators and a water supply system. There was also a chapel, a cinema and recreation buildings in addition to an Olympic size swimming pool. As there were no married quarters, some wives and families rented houses/apartments in Adelaide.

Maralinga had full airport facilities with the runway 7,217 feet [2.2 km] long to accommodate Royal Air Force aircraft including fully loaded Vickers Valiant and Avro Vulcan heavy bombers. Airlines of South Australia provided a Douglas DC-3 service from Adelaide via Woomera three times a week to bring in supplies, especially fresh food, and to provide transport for senior officers and NCOs. When going on leave, most personnel travelled by train with their fares paid by the AWRE.

The Range Commander of the Atomic Weapons Research Establishment was always a senior Australian officer with the deputy commander a British officer. At the height of the tests, in addition to a multitude of scientists, there were approximately 2000 military personnel from all three services of both nations.

The Australian Army was responsible for administration, motor transport and security; the British Royal Electrical and Mechanical Engineers [REME} provided vehicle maintenance. Both the Royal Air Force and the Royal Australian Air Force were responsible for air traffic control and maintaining airport facilities. The Royal Navy was responsible for electricity supply and the Royal Australian Navy was responsible for water supply which involved the distillation of water from artesian bores. Interestingly, one bore sunk to 90 feet deep was a few metres from an attempted well that explorer William Tietkens abandoned after sinking a shaft by hand to 50 feet in 1889

The last major underground test took place in March 1962 with several minor nuclear and conventional weapon tests taking place into 1963, so by the time I made my first visit, Maralinga was in assessment and clean up mode. However, with several scientists and military personal numbering around 400-500, it was still a considerable establishment.

As I have already written, I made my first weekend visit to Maralinga in June 1964 and was well accepted with 30-40 men at the service of Holy Communion. After discussion with the CO and his deputy, we decided that when I did a Land Rover patrol, I would make a 3-5 day visit which would allow extended time at the base. On these visits, I had time to meet personnel where they were working and after the initial visit I made it known that I would be in the chapel for 2-3 hours each morning if men wanted to talk. That ministry became so valuable that on successive visits, it was necessary to have appointments.

On these extended visits I went out to the test area with some of the officers which was fascinating experience. Travel to the test area was along the bitumen road; return to the village was along an unsealed road, known as the "Dirty Track" about 50 metres away from the main road. Before vehicles re-entered the village area, they were washed down to remove any radioactive particles. One thing that amazed me was the site of the last underground test where there was a hole about 150 feet across, and 120 feet deep with a silicacised rim about 5 feet high; an awesome example of the power of nuclear energy.

The extended visits to Maralinga were also beneficial for the Bush Church Aid Society. The CO of the REME suggested that they service the Land Rover when I visited, the only non-military vehicle allowed on site. This meant a huge saving of time and money because I would no longer need to take the vehicle to Port Augusta or even Adelaide for maintenance. It was agreed that manpower would cost nothing but we would pay for parts. There were two occasions in 1965 when the Land Rover needed repairs.

The first problem occurred when I was in the sandhills between Barton and Immarna. The transfer box started to leak oil. In that situation it was a disaster as I would not be able to change to four wheel drive and climb the sandhills. I got in touch with Maralinga through VKB and was told to get the vehicle to Watson by train where a recovery vehicle they would collect it. That meant getting a flat top wagon. Over the phone line, I called the train controller who told me nothing would be available for 24-48 hours.

In the afternoon. he discovered there was an empty wagon at Tarcoola and called the ganger with the news that it would be attached to the next day's Fast Goods The Immarna gang built a ramp and platform of old sleepers so I could get the vehicle on board when the train arrived. We were told the train could only stop for 10-15 minutes. However, the operation went without a hitch and the 'Rover" went to Maralinga where a new plug was fitted while I made my planned four-day visit.

The second need was replacement of a rear axle which broke as I was driving to the railway station at Tarcoola to collect a parcel. I contacted Maralinga and arranged for the Land Rover to be collected at Watson. Jeff Bolitho organised a flat top and I was able to use front wheel drive to get on to the loading platform and the wagon. I took Sunday services at Tarcoola and boarded the express early on Monday morning for Watson where a staff car was waiting for me on arrival. When I went down to the REME workshop and asked the CO how much the repair would cost, he laughed and said, "No cost, Padre", to which I responded, "'Come on Stan, we pay for parts". He replied, "Yes, well, we went out to the test area and cannibalised one of the Land Rovers left there". I said, "You mean to tell me I now have a radioactive axle". He laughed and replied, "I don't think so, Padre, but if it glows green in the dark, leave it where it is".

The extended ministry at Maralinga was fruitful and very satisfying. I had some great spiritual discussions in the officers' mess at night and made several friends, some of whom I was to meet at other bases when I became a Regular Army chaplain.

13.

THE SECOND YEAR AT TARCOOLA

Ministry in the second year of the Tarcoola Mission District followed the routine that had already been established. There were regular services and pastoral ministry at Tarcoola with fortnightly visits to Kingoonya for school classes and a lunch hour service at the hotel. There were monthly visits to Cook and Maralinga. There were three Land Rover patrols to Kalgoorlie and Welfare Car trips before Easter and Christmas which meant Jan could come. There were regular visits to the sheep/cattle stations.

However, other events which took place are worth mentioning.

The first of these was the children's camp at Smoky Bay in early January which was a wonderful success. A carriage was attached to the Fast Goods at Parkeston and made its first stop at Zanthus where some of the kids and two mothers to supervise joined the train. Further pickups were made at the other camps where there were children and as the train left Watson there were twenty kids on board. A few children from Tarcoola were taken by road.

Earlier, I had driven to Adelaide to pick up Jan's cousin, Amanda, and her friend Philippa, who had come for a holiday as well as to help at the camp. With Jan, Michael, Mandy, Philippa and *Snoopy* I drove to Smoky Bay and left them before going to Ooldea ahead of the bus. The train arrived, the children disembarked and we were off on the big adventure. The mothers went on to Barton where they could stay at the rest house and wait for their return train. At Ceduna, I picked up my cousin, Anne, who also came to assist, and went on to Smoky Bay. After the bus had dropped the kids off, we got them settled in their rooms before we took them for a swim/paddle in the shallow water. For some, it was the first time they had seen the sea and it was so exciting for them. That evening after dinner we played games on the beach.

On each of the five full days there was a Bible study led by Harry Goodhew, swimming classes, camp craft classes, games on the beach and visits to local spots including Point Lebatt where the kids were able to walk among the seals, picture nights and a bonfire on the beach.

Then it was time for the campers to return home. I dropped Jan, Michael, Anne and *Snoopy* at Ceduna where I waited for the bus to come from Smoky Bay. Then, going ahead of the bus with Mandy and Philippa, I headed for Ooldea and the train which arrived on time. Joining the train with the girls, we travelled with the children to Loongana where two mothers were waiting, as was the eastbound Fast Goods which we boarded for our return journey. We had a long stop at Cook before going on to Ooldea, the Land Rover and Ceduna.

In early February, Ken Dixon arrived to take over Tarcoola school. In his early 40s, Ken was a single man with a Church of Christ background. In his younger years he had begun theological training but during second year his fiancée was killed in a car accident and Ken lost his passion. He left the college and went back teaching. While he still attended church, his faith had been shaken.

Ken's forebears had been foundation members of the Church of Christ in Adelaide and when he arrived at Tarcoola, he was not sure whether he wanted to attend a church which was pastored by a Church of England minister. However, he put his doubts aside and began to attend both church and the weekly Bible study. One Saturday afternoon in Lent as I was preparing a sermon, Ken came and asked, "What does the Church of England teach about original sin?" I opened two Prayer Books and read Article IX with him before giving him W.H. Griffith Thomas's commentary on the Articles. Ken sat down on the floor of my study for nearly an hour as he read it. When he had finished, he said, "Original sin **is** a biblical doctrine! What is the next step for me to become a member of the Church of England?" We talked about confirmation and he agreed to join a preparation class along with four other townsfolk. They were confirmed during the year but more about that later.

In mid-April, Jan and I with Michael travelled to Cook on the passenger express for what could be best described as a celebrity occasion; the first wedding at Cook in 18 years. The sisters and I had spent some months preparing Floris Marks and Ronald [Mike] Howe for their marriage. In the week after the wedding there were reports in both Port Augusta's newspaper *The Transcontinental* and *The Kalgoorlie Miner*.

Handing Floris and Mike the Wedding Certificate

The Transcontinental Report

THE SECOND YEAR AT TARCOOLA

Jan wrote an article for the June issue of BCA journal entitled "Nullarbor Nuptial"–

> *The sun was shining, a cool breeze was blowing; everything seemed quiet and still as we arrived at Cook by train – but this was a false impression. There was busy preparation behind the closed doors of the 'sleepy looking' houses. This was the day of THE wedding– the first wedding at Cook since 1947.*
>
> *We went across to the hospital to find everything spic and span. The dining room was filled with bowls of fresh flowers sent from Kalgoorlie, 539 miles away. What a rare and lovely sight they were here! Roses, dahlias, zinnias and others, all beautifully arranged. This room, with chairs from all over town neatly placed, was to be the 'chapel'. The adjoining room, a hospital ward, was to be the vestry while the veranda was furnished with chairs and a long table which was set for afternoon tea.*
>
> *As the time approached - 3:30pm - the chapel was filled to overflowing with the excited townsfolk dressed in their very best.*
>
> *At 3:45, to the strains of the Bridal March from Lohengrin, the bride, dressed in a lovely white nylon frock made by the porter's wife entered the chapel on the arm of the stationmaster. She was preceded by a flower girl and a young bridesmaid.*
>
> *The ceremony was completed with only one hitch – quite some difficulty in getting the ring on that third finger.*
>
> *Then with photos taken outside, confetti everywhere, the guests went into a lovely afternoon tea. A beautiful white wedding cake made by Sister Ross and decorated by Margaret Reid, the stationmaster's wife, graced the centre of the table.*

The food was eaten, the toast and speeches made, and everyone had a lot of fun. Children and parents then wended their way home – the children to bed, with most of the parents to return for Evening Prayer.

The bride and groom joined us in worshipping God that evening. What a wonderful end to such a happy day and what a wonderful way to start married life!

At the end of May, Tarcoola was the venue for the quarterly Rural Deanery chapter meeting when the clergy from all parishes on Eyre Peninsula came together for fellowship and discussion. Travel to this gathering was different as usually we all drove to the venue. However, except for Minnipa and Ceduna, Tarcoola was 300-500 miles from the other parishes.

Only Harry Goodhew drove to Tarcoola, picking up the priest-in-charge of Minnipa on the way. The others drove to Port Augusta where I had arranged for a carriage to be attached to the Fast Goods to transport them and for accommodation at Tarcoola. It was a fun trip because instead of gathering in a parish church, they said Evening Prayer on the train. There was much merriment from those on the bottom bunks as they read the set Psalm, 147 with verse 10 – "*He (God) taketh not pleasure in the legs of a man*" with the legs of those on top bunks dangling in front of them.

The train arrived at 7:30am and everybody, including three wives, came across to the Rectory for breakfast. The meeting got underway at 10:30 with a break for lunch after which there was a walk around town, including a visit to the hospital. We had Evensong in the church, followed by dinner at the hospital and further discussion.

We reconvened after breakfast the next morning to continue the meeting. After lunch, with the few cars in town, we took everyone on a tour of the old gold mining town. Then, after a quick evening meal, it was back to the railway station. The carriage was attached to the east bound Fast Goods. Farewells were made and the visitors boarded the carriage. The train pulled out slowly with the driver vigorously sounding the horn and all the locals waving. However, if the journey to Tarcoola was fun, the return journey was hilarious. But more of that in a later chapter.

Barbara Fox was transferred from Cook to Tarcoola in June.

The Bishop of Adelaide, The Rt Revd Thomas Reed, arrived on the passenger express early in the morning of the first Saturday in July to confirm the five local candidates and two adults from Ceduna. It was a difficult weekend with the bishop totally out of his comfort zone in this "frontier" town. After breakfast, he spent the morning walking around town in a purple cassock and not one person spoke to him. Indeed, as they saw him coming, they scurried into their houses and many of them asked me after the weekend, "Who was that funny man in the purple dress who stayed with you?" I had to explain that he was the bishop.

Bishop Reed was rather grumpy for the rest of the day although he sparked up when we went to the hospital for dinner. Still grumpy the next morning, as I welcomed him at the 8 o'clock service, he snarled, "There's no need to welcome me. I'm the bishop of the diocese". He preached at the service, took the Confirmation in the afternoon and sat in the congregation in the evening when he seemed more relaxed, possibly because he was heading back to Adelaide early in the morning. The express was running early on Monday so I had him up at 3:00am.

Despite it being a difficult weekend, it must have impacted on him because when I put my hand up to move an amendment to a motion at synod in August, he gave me the call. As I walked to a microphone, he announced, "The Priest-in-Charge of Tarcoola, who probably has the most difficult task of any priest in the diocese".

We were delighted when, in August, Ken Dixon and Marge Tarr announced their engagement with the wedding to take place in Sydney in January. Watching their relationship develop and looking back, one can see the amazing hand of God in that with Marge's transfer from Cook to Tarcoola earlier in the year before Ken's appointment as schoolteacher.

In September, Commonwealth Railways Commissioner, Keith Smith made his triennial visit along the Line by special train which consisted of his carriage with bedrooms and lounge room together with a dining car and kitchen. The train was stabled at Tarcoola for two days during which we and the Sisters were invited to dinner.

Keith was accompanied by a Japanese businessman, the managing director of one of the big electronic companies. During the meal, Keith talked with me about the ministry and asked, "What would make your work easier?". I responded, "I'd love a lightweight 12-volt generator". Keith turned to the Japanese man and said, "You could supply that, couldn't you?" Some weeks later, in time for the last patrol of the year, a new compact generator with a carrying handle arrived. It weighed 40lbs [18 kg] - about a third the weight of the old monster.

Before the last Land Rover patrol of the year took place in October/November, I realised that by the time I had finished the trip, the vehicle would have over 29,000 miles on the odometer and would need to have the pre-end of warranty service which could only be done at a Land Rover distributor. What to do? I could rail the Land Rover back to Tarcoola after the patrol and then drive to Adelaide – 300 miles of dirt and 200 miles of sealed road or I could drive to Perth on sealed roads. I chose the latter option.

Major Gordon Nicol, the senior administrative officer at Maralinga took some leave and joined me. Gordon had become a good friend and had wanted to do the trip for twelve months. He had spent two years at a Dominican seminary before joining the army during the Korean War. He was great company and a wonderful help when we got bogged to the axle outside Cook as heavy rain, 2 inches [51mm] in 1½ hours, caused a flood.

At Kalgoorlie we stayed with the bishop and Peggy. Jan left *Snoopy* with Ken and the following evening arrived with Michael on the express. We had another night at Bishopsbourne before heading for Perth - a four day trip via Norseman, Esperance, Albany, Manjimup and Bunbury. In Perth, we stayed at a hotel as guests of the owner, whose daughter Pauline was engaged to Billy Robins of Kychering station just north of Tarcoola.

While the Land Rover was being serviced, I had the opportunity to preach at a lunch hour service in St George's Cathedral where my friend Jim Payne was the Dean. After we arrived back at Kalgoorlie. I took the vehicle to Parkeston and loaded it onto a flat top wagon before Gordon, Jan, Michael and I left on the express for Watson and Tarcoola.

If I thought that was the end of the year apart from Welfare Car and station trips how mistaken I was!

A week after we got home from Perth, there was a message from Bill Rich via VKB that he wanted to see me in Adelaide in three days' time when he made a stopover on the way to Geraldton. The message told me that pilot Alan Chadwick would fly to Tarcoola in the Cessna with Harry Goodhew and Matron Marion Hope and take the three of us to Adelaide.

I had an hour alone with Bill during which he told me that the Bishop of Kalgoorlie wanted the Society to provide a priest for Norseman, which included the Eyre Highway sheep stations as far east to Eucla. Bill told me he had suggested to Bishop Cecil that I take up the appointment and the bishop was enthusiastic about that. I thought what a pity we had not known about this before we stopped at Norseman for refreshments a few weeks earlier. Our move to Norseman would be next June, which would enable me to visit the stations, do a Land Rover patrol, including Maralinga and for us to do a farewell Welfare Car trip before Easter.

14.

PREPARING TO MOVE

After three years in the field, BCA paid for travel back home for furlough, so just after Christmas we drove to Adelaide and left the Land Rover with the Revd Peter Newall who was going to act as locum at Tarcoola for three Sundays.

Our year began with a holiday in Sydney and Newcastle so we could spend time with our mothers and relax. An added incentive to go east was the wedding of Ken Dixon and Marge Tarr at St Paul's Chatswood in the middle of our holiday. I had the privilege of being Ken's best man on this joyous occasion. Ken and Marge returned to Tarcoola before the school year began and while Marge had retired, she remained on call for emergencies.

At the end of January, there were Commonwealth Railways staff changes. Dave Reid was transferred to Kalgoorlie as Stationmaster [Passenger]; Jeff Bolitho was appointed Assistant Stationmaster [Goods] with responsibility for Parkeston.

In early February I undertook my last station visits followed by the last Land Rover patrol to Kalgoorlie There was sadness because while we would do a Welfare Car trip before Easter, I was saying goodbye to my parishioners.

PREPARING TO MOVE

In mid-March Sister Rosemary Bond arrived at Tarcoola to assist Barbara Fox who had been on her own at the hospital following Marge Dixon's retirement. Rosemary wrote:

> *"I will never forget the trip in the Flying Doctor's plane, looking out over the vast landscape of endless sand hills and salt lakes, then seeing a long straight railway line with twenty houses clustered alongside,*

When the plane arrived, I wandered up to the hospital to see everybody and I have a great memory of Rosemary's reaction when I walked in the door. She cried out, "John!" rushed towards me and threw her arms around me which rather surprised matron Marion Hope. I had known Rosemary as a teenage member of the youth fellowship at All Saints Balgowlah and to have somebody she knew in this isolated place eased her anxiety.

With Easter on 10 April, Jan and I with Michael and *Snoopy* did our last trip in the Welfare Car. Again, there was a lot of sadness and a few tears, even from hardened fettlers. When Paddy at 757 Mile camp said to me as I reboarded the train, "I'll miss you Padre; you have given me hope", I realised that the ministry had been more fruitful than I had thought. Even though the women had only seen Jan a couple of times each year, they also told her that they would miss her.

Back at Tarcoola, Ken Dixon and I walked across to the church on Maundy Thursday to prepare it for the weekend. On pushing the door open, we were confronted with the sight of two sheets of the fibro ceiling having collapsed under the weight of almost fifty years of sandstorms. We devised an ingenious plan with two vacuum cleaners sucking the sand out through the windows, washing the pews and then dusting everything down. It took us about four hours.

I made my last visit to Maralinga after Easter and then began the task of packing up our personal effects which would go with us to Norseman while the furniture would remain for our successors.

I wrote to Commissioner Keith Smith to thank him for the generous assistance Commonwealth Railways had given us. His response was to say that he felt he was the one who should say "thank you because your ministry has made all the railway workers and their families much more contented people". With his letter he enclosed a first class pass to Alice Springs and return with an extension to Kalgoorlie. As a result, we had a wonderful trip on the *Ghan* with free travel to Kalgoorlie.

This was the old *Ghan* which travelled through Quorn on the standard gauge track to Maree before passengers and their luggage were transferred to the narrow 3' 6" railway line for the remainder of the journey during which the trains probably travelled at a maximum of 25 mph [40kph]. In many places, like the Finke River crossing, the track was laid on the sand without any ballast. In fact, the turning triangle was laid up the dry river bed and so was easy to replace after a flood.

Not only extending our return journey to Kalgoorlie, Commonwealth Railways provided a goods wagon to take our possessions to the West free of charge. We packed the wagon before we left for the Alice and it remained at the siding until the day before we passed through Tarcoola on the way to Kal. Our journey on the *Ghan* was a wonderful experience. I knew most the crew because they also staffed the trains on the Trans Line and they treated us like royalty.

At Alice Springs we stayed with John and Elaine Pemberthy. John was the teacher of the School of the Air, a role he had previously fulfilled in Ceduna via VKB. He was one of the confirmees that Harry Goodhew brought to Tarcoola in 1965. Elaine was the night nurse at Ceduna when Michael was born.

PREPARING TO MOVE

The Schools of the Air provided primary and early secondary education for children in remote areas of Australia such as the sheep/cattle stations. Each student had direct contact with a teacher in an inland town, typically spending one hour per day receiving group or individual lessons over the radio from the teacher and the rest of the day working through the assigned materials with a parent or older sibling.

Originally, the students received their course materials and returned their written work/projects to their hub centre through the Flying Doctor Services or by mail. As they were in isolated situations, the School of the Air was frequently their first chance to socialise with children outside their immediate family. This was supplemented by gatherings each year when the children travelled to the school centre to spend a week with their teacher and classmates. Studies have shown that such education is on par with, if not better than, standards set by the traditional methods of schooling[43].

15.
WHAT HAPPENED NEXT

A month or so after we left Tarcoola, Revd Brian Carter with his wife Carolyn arrived in Tarcoola to continue the ministry until Brian was appointed priest-in-charge of Leigh Creek in 1969.

Brian's first trip along the Line was rather dramatic!

He used the Welfare Car attached to the *Tea and Sugar* with the short stops at all the camps so he could introduce himself. It was good idea but ended disastrously. At Zanthus the driver sounded the horn as usual to warn people that the train was leaving in fifteen minutes. Thinking the train was about to depart immediately, Brian ran towards it and in the dark ran into a stack of rails, fracturing his kneecap.

He was transported to Parkeston on the train where an ambulance was waiting to take him to Kalgoorlie Hospital. Jeff Bolitho phoned me at Norseman with the news and I immediately headed for Kalgoorlie in the late afternoon. At the hospital, I was told that Brian would be in hospital for a few days so I decided to stay in Kal. I think I got in touch with the hospital at Tarcoola to get a message to Carolyn.

At 5:30pm, I drafted a message for the BCA office in Sydney which I dictated to the telegram office forgetting the two hour time difference.

WHAT HAPPENED NEXT

The message read, *Brian Carter in Kalgoorlie Hospital with fractured knee. Contact me at Bishopsbourne.* Of course, at 7:30pm, the office was closed and the telegram was not delivered until the next morning.

Just after 7:00am, WA time, I had a phone call from a frantic Bill Rich. "How is Brian? Is he paralysed?" I responded, "What?" Bill said, with panic in his voice, "We got the telegram, *Brian Carter in hospital with fractured neck.*" I replied, "Oh no! The dictated message was "with fractured knee". It took me some time to calm Bill down. I stayed in Kalgoorlie for a couple of more nights and then saw Brian safely settled on the express for his return trip to Tarcoola.

During his time at Tarcoola, Brian led Murray Abinett, Jeff Bolitho's successor as stationmaster, to the Lord

By the time Brian was transferred to Leigh Creek in 1969, Coober Pedy had become a new district and the missioner there took over the responsibility for the northern sheep/cattle stations, the first of which was only 30 miles [48km] south of the town. It was decided not to have a resident minister at Tarcoola.

In the same year, the Revd Ray Neve who had served Ceduna, Wilcannia and Menindee was appointed Rector of Kambalda, the nickel mining town south of Kalgoorlie. Ray picked up the responsibility of the Western Australia section of the Trans Line ministry and undertook 1-2 trips a year in the Welfare Car until he moved to Norseman in 1971. He probably went to Rawlinna and east of the border to Cook. I do not know whether Ray went further east to Barton.

The Revd Ralph Holden who was the priest-in-charge of Cummins, 67 km north of Port Lincoln. picked up the responsibility of visiting the southern sheep stations in the former Tarcoola Mission District as well as Kingoonya and Tarcoola once a quarter as a parish outreach. He did this for several years by which time railway staff numbers were being reduced. I do not know if Ralph ever went to Cook.

16.

SOME REFLECTIONS

In addition to the isolation and need to plan our weekly shopping there was the temperature, dust storms and a flood.

In summer, the temperature frequently reached 120ºF [49ºC] while in winter it was necessary to have a fire burning because of the cold. Air-conditioning, apart from a water cooler, was non-existent. There was no air-conditioning in the Land Rover either. When I read today's weather reports sensationally telling us parts of South Australia are experiencing temperatures around 50°C, I am amused. The young journalists have no idea!

We experienced one major dust storm while we were living at Tarcoola. It blanketed the town and filled houses. Years later we opened a pack of sheets we had been given as a wedding present and never used. Despite it being sealed there were grains of red sand in the folds

The flood in 1964 was unexpected and there was no warning. 3½ inches [87.5 mm] fell in one and a half hours and the water poured down from the hill above town. I had gone to Port Augusta to do some banking and other business, leaving Tarcoola on the express at 4 30am. The train arrived in Port at 11 o'clock giving me six hours to do everything before

SOME REFLECTIONS

the westbound express departed at 5:00pm. After dinner I sat in the lounge car chatting with other passengers until they drifted off to their cabins. As the train travelled west of Pimba, I was entertained by almost continuous lightning strikes to the south.

The train arrived at Tarcoola on time at 12.30am and as I was about to get into the Land Rover which I had left at the station, there was a simultaneous crash of thunder and lightning strike on the police station radio aerial. I drove to the house in pelting rain and as I went through the back gate, I realised that the yard was flooded. *Snoopy*, tied up at the back door, was drenched and his kennel had floated away. He was very glad to see me.

Jan slept through it all and only woke when I came into the house. She got up and we went to the front door to see that the water was about an inch below the floorboards pouring across the road and the railway line. We wrapped Michael up and drove to the hospital to make sure the girls were OK.

In the morning, there was debris everywhere. The road was flooded and the railway line was underwater with a goods train stranded. It was with us for two days The passenger express had been stopped at Barton. The kids were out paddling with youngest ones never having seen rain before.

There was an interesting sideline to the flood. When I first visited Tarcoola in 1963, I wondered why there was a 50 cm high brick wall around the repeater station with a ramp on either side to allow equipment to be brought in or taken out. Puzzled, I asked, "What on earth is that wall for" and received the reply, "To protect the equipment from floods." I was rather disbelieving that a flood was possible. Ah well, the builders knew best.

One night there was a drama. Dr Mueller decided to fly up to Tarcoola because of a medical emergency that was deemed too serious for the sisters to handle on their own. People in town and nearby stations were woken up so they could park vehicles along the sides of the airstrip with headlights on. They also had to keep the inquisitive kangaroos at bay, as the car lights attracted them. Once the plane safely landed, it taxied up to the back door of the hospital and Merna was greeted with much relief.

It was at times like this that you realised what great medical services BCA and the RFDS[44] provided for the people in the bush.

17.
FURTHER REMINISCENCES

There were occasions of joy, of sadness and regret during our time on the Line.

Apart from The Wedding already mentioned. We had the joy of being accepted by the people in all the camps, because living at Tarcoola, we were treated as one of them. The women loved having Jan visit 2-3 times a year. At each settlement where I stayed overnight there was nearly 100% attendance, even though they knew there would be a Gospel film and message. Pastors in cities and towns only dream about this.

Jeff Bolitho's conversion led to a total life change. He had previously been aggressive and angry, especially when he got drunk. Train crews spent as little time as possible in the station office because of his attitude. He stopped drinking and after that train crews loved to come in and talk with him because of his experience along the Line, initially as a shunter. Towards the end of 1965, he applied for the vacant position of stationmaster at Port Augusta. The Chief Traffic Manager made a special trip to Tarcoola to tell him face-to-face that the appointment was being given to somebody else but added that a new position of Assistant Stationmaster [Goods] had been created at Kalgoorlie and because of the change in his attitude, the appointment was his if he applied for it.

There was further joy before I left Tarcoola when Ken Dixon told me that his passion for ministry had been revived and he had applied to go to theological college in 1967. He enrolled at St Barnabas College and was subsequently ordained in the Diocese of Adelaide.

There was the sadness of the only funeral I had during my time on the Trans Line. Jack, a fettler with the Mount Christie single men's gang, died of a heart attack while I was on a weekend visit to Cook. Jack seemingly had no next of kin and his chosen surname was only known at the Commonwealth Railways office in Port Augusta. His body was brought to Tarcoola and prepared for burial at the hospital after policeman Ray Wandel, who was both coroner and undertaker, had certified that he had died.

When I returned from Cook in the late afternoon on the Fast Goods, Ken Dixon met and greeted me, "You've got a funeral tomorrow morning". When I said, 'Who' he replied, "I don't know." The funeral did not take place until 2:30pm as the two fettlers digging a grave in the old goldfields cemetery had difficulty because it was mostly limestone. Eventually a stick of gelignite was used.

The sadness was in the fact that the only people who took part in the service were the two fettlers, Ray Wandel and me. None of his workmates from Mt Christie came After the brief ceremony, the four of us filled in the grave.

My biggest regret was not giving enough time to Jan because of ministry demands. I did not allow for the loneliness she experienced when I was on patrol. She was the only young mum in Tarcoola and while she had the fellowship of the BCA sisters and the other Christians, it was not the same as it would have been had I been home. Looking back, we estimate that I spent the equivalent of seven months of the year away which was not good in the first year for a newly married couple with a newborn child. As mentioned in an earlier chapter, it was a similar experience for Bernard and Coralie Buckland. Of course, the perceived responsibility of ministry affects clergy families in the city as well.

In my later years of ministry, I drew up a list of priorities for the pastor which I used in seminars and teaching missions. It resulted in a lot of discussion, sometimes anger and the need for explanation. However, I believe these priorities are right and in accordance with Scripture.

Consider Deuteronomy 24:5 - *If a man has recently married, he must not be sent to war or have any other duty laid on him. For one year he is to be free to stay at home and bring happiness to the wife he has married.*

That does not mean he does not work but essentially says he is to spend as much time at home as is possible.

The priorities are:

1. God, including Prayer
2. Wife & Children
3. Study, including Preparation
4. Leaders
5. The Congregation

Back in Sydney, Jan and I began to do the weekly shopping together; a practice we have continued to the present day. Saturday was spent transporting the kids to sport and watching their games even if it meant missing out on seminars and other meetings. We had regular holidays, camping or staying in the holiday homes of friends. I used to meet the churchwardens for lunch in the locations where they worked every couple of months. Interestingly, putting the above priorities into practice as best I could, I seemed to have more time for the congregation.

18.

AND, THERE WAS HUMOUR

The two funniest memories are the return trip to Port Augusta for my colleagues after the Rural Deanery meeting and a radio conversation with VKB while on patrol across the Nullabor.

As the train pulled slowly out of Tarcoola yard, the carriage with the clergy and wives behind the two locos, Jan and I returned to the Land Rover and discovered there was a jacket hanging over the passenger seat. It was rural dean John Meakin's coat. What to do?

With the train moving very slowly, I decided to drive the 20 km to the crossing at Wilgena sheep station as the train would not have gathered full speed and it might be possible to stop it. We parked the Land Rover beside the railway line and as the train approached, Jan pumped the brake pedal so that the taillights would flash. Red lights are the signal to a driver to stop. I jumped out of the vehicle and held the coat up. It was all to no avail. As the train approached, seeing the red light, the driver, who was a good friend, started to slow down. Then seeing it was me and thinking that it was an extension of the farewell, he opened the throttle and the train gathered speed.

As the train sped past, horn blowing, his companions told me later that seeing what I was holding up, John Meakin, cried out, "My coat!" That was

AND, THERE WAS HUMOUR

followed by another exclamation, "My wallet" and then. "My car keys!" There was nothing else to do but return to Tarcoola and pack the coat in a box addressed to Revd John Meakin, Port Augusta so it could be given to the guard when the passenger express arrived at 4:30 in the morning and taken to Port where John would be waiting.

However, that was not the end of the story.

The clergy and wives, except for priest in charge of Woomera, Keith Chittleborough, went to their cabins. Keith dozed in the lounge area because he was leaving the train at Pimba. Three hours into the journey, wondering if the lights of Woomera would be visible, Keith went out on the open platform at the front of the carriage. The door slammed behind him. There was no handle on the outside and he could not get back inside. He banged on the door and shouted which woke one of his colleagues. Bleary eyed, this man came to the door, saw Keith outside and his bag inside. He opened the door, put the suitcase out and shut the door again. Keith had no alternative but to wait outside for another half-hour with a cold wind whistling past. The story made the newspaper *The Anglican*.

The second incident occurred on the Nullarbor Plain.

Arriving at Cook and trying to avoid a large rock in the middle of the street. I managed to slash the inside of a tyre on another sharp rock. Then two days later near the border, I had a blowout and was left with no spares. I knew there was equipment to replace tyres at Forrest airport, about 100 miles away, so decided to have two tyres and tubes sent there. I waited until the VKB Ceduna 10:00am schedule so I could send a telegram to the Land Rover agent in Kalgoorlie. Kevin Ellis was the radio operator. The conversation went like this:

> 9TG Portable:
> "Kevin, I want to send a telegram. Over".

VKB:
"Go ahead John. Over"

I dictated the first part of the message and switched to 'Receive'.

VKB:
"John, I'm having difficulty hearing you clearly. Are you using your whip aerial or an outside aerial? Over"'

The whip aerial was telescopic and attached to the Land Rover; the outside aerial was a length of wire slung over the branch of a tree and often better for transmission during the middle of and late in the day.

9TG Portable:
"Kevin, I am using my whip aerial. Over":

VKB:
"John, could you throw your outside aerial over a branch. Over."

I looked to the north, to the south, to the east, to the west and at *Snoopy*, who was sitting at the steering wheel. I shook my head and switched to 'Transmit'

9TG Portable:
"Kevin, I am in the middle of the Nullabor Plain. I haven't seen a tree for nearly a week and neither has *Snoopy*. He is nearly frantic! I'll dictate slowly, read it back and send it please. Over"

The telegram was sent, the tyres arrived at Forrest and repairs were done.

AND, THERE WAS HUMOUR

Eight weeks later, I was doing a northern station patrol. When I arrived at Billa Kalina, Colin Greenfield came out the door of the homestead and as I was getting out, greeted me, "G'day mate, how are things?" He turned to *Snoopy*, patted him on the head and said, "Hullo *Snoopy*, have you found a tree yet?" I burst out laughing as I realised that probably everybody on the network had been listening in to the exchange between Kevin and me.

EPILOGUE

The Trans Australia Railway Line described in the foregoing pages is no more.

Of course, the railway line still exists and with the standardisation of the track from Broken Hill to Port Pirie and Adelaide, Kalgoorlie to Perth, means that it is now the standard gauge of 4' 8½" from Sydney to Perth. Added to that, the building of an all-weather standard gauge track to Alice Springs, extended to Darwin together with the standardisation of the railway line between Melbourne and Adelaide means all mainland capitals are connected without break of gauge. The junction for the North Australia Railway is Tarcoola and the points are changed remotely.

While the railway is mainly used for freight operations between the cities with trains anything up to 1.8 km long, there are two luxury passenger trains – the *Indian Pacific* between Sydney and Perth via Adelaide and *The Ghan* from Adelaide to Darwin. They operate once a week, sometimes twice in peak periods, in both directions. They often have up to 30 carriages.

Replacement of wooden sleepers with concrete ones and welded rail means there is no need for fettler gangs nor servicing facilities. The tracks are inspected regularly with special machines and maintenance is now undertaken by 'fly-in' teams. With no resident fettlers, the *Tea and Sugar* no longer operates and the houses in all the settlements have been demolished as have most of the houses at Kingoonya, Tarcoola, Cook and Rawlinna. The schools and the hospitals have also been demolished. Kingoonya and Tarcoola each have a few houses mainly used by mining exploration workers or tourists. The Kingoonya pub still exists and provides accommodation for four-wheel-drive enthusiasts.

Tarcoola has no permanent residents; Cook has a population of four responsible for refuelling locomotives which all stop there. During the stop, passengers on the *Indian Pacific* can get off the train and look around. One lock-up still exist as a tourist attraction. Rawlinna has a larger population serving the *Indian Pacific* which makes a stop so passengers can have a barbecue dinner in the outback. It also serves as the railhead for an enormous sheep/cattle station that was in its embryo stage when I served on the Line. Each train now has two crews who no longer end their shifts and stay at rest houses but have very comfortable sleeping accommodation on the trains.

While it is the end of an era in Australia's history, there are still some reminders with a couple of GMs, carriages and the butcher's van preserved at rail museums. In addition to that, a few GM locomotives are still operational with Southern Shorthaul Railway in New South Wales.

END NOTES

1. Much of this information is extracted from the Year Book Australia – 1918.
2. ibid
3. Personal knowledge of the author
4. ibid.
5. ibid
6. ibid
7. Australia Year Book 1918
8. Personal knowledge of the author.
9. ibid
10. "The Australian Railwayman" 2012
11. Postmaster General's Department which was responsible for telephone lines throughout Australia
12. Australian Broadcasting Commission. The landline between the Eastern states and Perth was established in 1933.
13. The ganger was the team foreman
14. *The Burra Record* 10 July 1901
15. ibid
16. ibid
17. ibid
18. The Advertiser 12 August 1902
19. The Advertiser 12 August 1902
20. The Advertiser 21 August 1902
21. Personal knowledge of the author
22. Conveyed to the author by Mr Keith Smith, the Commissioner for Commonwealth Railways during a visit to Tarcoola in 1965.
23. Personal knowledge of the author who has copies of some of them.
24. Revd H Broadley – Letter to the West Coast Sentinel, Ceduna SA, c 1930

25 "These Ten Years" – Revd S. J Kirkby 1930;
"These Twenty Years" - Revd T.E Jones 1939;
"Australian Outback – Helen Caterer 1982.
"BCA 75 Not Out 1919-1994" – Editor: Revd Peter George 1994
"Fox Tales from Far Flung Places" – Barbara Fox 2003
"Stout Hearts for Steep Hills" – Joy Brann, AM 2009
"Never too Far, Never to Few" – Robyn Powell 2019
26 Wife of Major-General Sir Winston Dugan, Governor of South Australia 1934-1939
27 "BCA 75 Not Out 1919-1994" – Editor: Revd Peter George 1994
28 This was told to the author by Betty Churches of Kokatha station
29 Philip regularly wrote letters of encouragement to me.
30 The guard's van which was located between the locomotive and the kitchen carriage.
31 1½ hours behind South Australia
32 I always wore my collar when travelling on the Passenger train as it opened the way for conversation.
33 Church of England Boys' Society, a uniformed organisation like Cubs and Scouts
34 The Dingo is the Australian native wild dog which created havoc among the sheep flocks
35 A cup of tea
36 Citizens' Military Force, now the Army Reserve,
37 There were five refueling stops from Sydney - Mildura, Adelaide, Ceduna, Forrest and Kalgoorlie. The trip took two days.
38 Royal Australian Air Force
39 Bob was chaplain at Pulteney Grammar School
40 A large pothole full of powdered red/brown sand. This one was probably 10-15cm deep and twice the length of the Land Rover.
41 That was rectified in December when two months stipend was paid
42 Genesis 22:14
43 Imamura, E (1987). In Conventional and nonconventional schooling: a comparison of pupil performance in rural schools and schools of the air. University of Western Australia
44 Royal Flying Doctor Service

www.ingramcontent.com/pod-product-compliance
Lightning Source LLC
LaVergne TN
LVHW021410080426
835508LV00020B/2541